Overcoming Solidity

Overcoming Solidity

World Crisis and the New Nature

John C. Woodcock

iUniverse, Inc.
Bloomington

Overcoming Solidity
World Crisis and the New Nature

iUniverse books may be ordered through booksellers or by contacting:

iUniverse
1663 Liberty Drive
Bloomington, IN 47403
www.iuniverse.com
1-800-Authors (1-800-288-4677)

ISBN: 978-1-4759-8376-0 (sc)
ISBN: 978-1-4759-8377-7 (ebk)

Printed in the United States of America

iUniverse rev. date: 04/03/2013

Cover. Graue Steine by AlterFalter: http://us.fotolia.com/id/39464127

Contents

ACKNOWLEDGEMENT

With gratitude to Wolfgang Giegerich who taught me the courage to think a thought (as it thinks itself out through me) to the end.

This is what is meant today by:

entering the wild . . .

Without raising into consciousness the subliminal logic [i.e., the logos, living thinking—my insert] *inherent in our perceiving today; without the painful effort of, step by step, reconstructing in our frame of mind the history of logical transmutations that is condensed and collapsed into the things of our modern world and preserved in them, we are more or less like the followers of the Melanesian cargo cult. They did not see what their cult was to a large extent about: technical things like airplanes, watches, radios etc. What they saw were objects conceived within an "animistic" or "mythological" consciousness, by which objects they supplanted the products brought into their world from without.*

Wolfgang Giegerich

We in the West are so placed that, as our self-consciousness increases, we feel: over there is the material world, all that I experience as sense perception . . . and over here is the "I" . . . and between the two there is no connection . . . . Then we begin to understand that another relation between the senses and the too acutely self-conscious Ego is possible . . . We go back now to all the richness and colour of the [ensouled world], *but in such a way that it is redeemed. Sense-perception has become spiritual perception.*

Owen Barfield

PREFACE

The intent of my book is to "put under a microscope" our very understandable responses to the wide-spread apprehension of an imminent world crisis. Although this feeling finds many expressions today, within many disciplines, I focus here on the philosophical/psychological stream of thought that speaks to a gulf between consciousness and world and the problem of overcoming that gulf—a response I describe as overcoming solidity. The presence of the gulf seems to evoke an impulse to overcome it, to return to earlier times when our relationship to nature was more participatory, more alive, more of an I-Thou relationship. There is a pervasive belief among proponents of this response that such a "re-enchantment" of nature will restore the lost connection, thereby reducing the exploitation and destruction of the natural world, along with the human species. Part of my purpose here is to demonstrate the impossibility and therefore futility of any such attempt. We must, I claim, accept the irreversibility of history but, alternatively, we do not have to accept the positivist prejudice that asserts the absolute nature of our current consciousness-world constitution.

I approach this issue from within the wisdom stream of philosophical/psychological thought that privileges the soul as a historical process in which revolutionary changes in the soul-world constitution occur. I (along with others) call this process the evolution of consciousness or, more accurately, the evolution of the consciousness-world constitution. I am claiming that the question of overcoming solidity only makes sense when explored from within this wisdom stream and even then, it is a complex and difficult issue to comprehend. The only way I could do any justice to the topic is to draw from many different sources, including my own experiences. In the course of my research, I discovered that I could make an important distinction between the possibility of individual experience in overcoming solidity, while remaining within our current status of soul-world (separated self-consciousness and world of solid things) *and* the possibility of the soul-world constitution undergoing another self-transformation, thereby overcoming its own present status.

I also offer hints of what such a self-transformation would look like, and here we run into great problems because now we are talking about the unknown future as it is forming. Such a process inevitably involves language as a vehicle of expression of the new status of soul-world and I explore this process in depth in my book: *Manifesting Possible Futures*. However, in this book I simply offer an image of the emergence of this possible future by reference to the "twice-born", Dionysos, appearing, not as the living truth of the ebullience and exuberance of living natural nature, but as the very syntax of a new dawning consciousness. From this tentative hypothesis I introduce the work, or artistic productions, including my own, of some individual human voices that seem to show the "presence" of the soul's transformation into its new status of "being", i.e., the "new nature".

INTRODUCTION

SUBLATE (aufheben). Also translated as 'supersede' and 'sublimate'. It incorporates the senses of:

(i) to cancel out, abolish, do away with, or reverse (a judgment),

(ii) to keep or preserve, and

(iii) to lift or raise up. Sublation connotes progress, by virtue of (i)-(iii): when something is sublated, it is not done away with but retained and preserved in the higher product which supersedes it.

Sublation involves mediation and (determinate) negation. Hegel speaks of both concepts and things as sublated.

(Hegel, 2013)

The key to everything I have to say here in this book lies in the concept of sublation.

We know that today we are divorced from nature to a degree that is threatening our existence. We also know that those sensual, animal qualities that characterized our existence, when we were embedded soulfully in nature, have departed and we long for their return. As D. H. Lawrence hoped:

"Cool, unlying life will rush in . . . and institutions will curl up like burnt paper." [1]

Lawrence apparently believed, along with many other intelligent and thoughtful pundits of our times, that such a return to nature is possible, literally. The usual argument, as we will see with the outstanding example of C. S. Lewis, is that we have arrived here, "in the glass bottle of our egos," through a series of missteps, leading us ineluctably away from the gifts of nature, that remain, as Lawrence indicates, waiting for us should we choose to return.

Except there is not one shred of evidence to indicate that such hopes or beliefs have any validity whatsoever, in theory, or in actual experience of our modern existence! They are nothing more than futile and idle nostalgia, as our existence accelerates its psychological distance from what I will call *natural nature* (for reasons that will become clear later on). This is so whether or not individual people or groups form associations for the purpose of practicing Lawrentian methods of "returning to nature". Such attempts only occur on islands within the juggernaut of our technological civilization that is strengthening its "monotheistic" vision on the world.

So this book is a refutation of such attempts. We must, I will claim, come to terms with the irrevocable loss of our embeddedness in natural nature with its "cool, unlying life rushing in, making our bodies taut with power!"

But is that all there is—acceptance of our present distance from these qualities of life, getting on the best we can? For many people the answer is clearly yes. Untroubled by any such thoughts as their own dissociation from natural nature (as human *animals*), many are simply diving unreservedly

---

[1]   From his poem, *Escape*.

into our modern world—that of our technological civilization and its *artificial nature*. Yet there are many who are so troubled and equally many who are offering a new way, such as D. H. Lawrence and C. S. Lewis.

My thesis here, as I said, utterly refutes such "new ways to return to the way things were" as futile and ignorant. Ignorant of what?! My refutation is rooted in a stream of thought, or better, a wisdom-stream, to which belongs the idea of the evolution of consciousness. Everything I have to say here rests on the reality of the evolution of consciousness, or more correctly, the evolution of the consciousness-world constitution—the way that soul and world are together simultaneously constituted. As *human* animals, we are always embedded within the necessities of a soul-world reality, which has undergone a series of transformations, changing both poles irrevocably. We humans suffer the consequences of this historical necessity. Our cultural forms and our empirical lives are greatly affected by how we respond to the historical transformations in the soul-world, but we are not the authors of such transformations. I will try to provide a brief discussion of the philosophical backing to these claims later but for now I want right-away to *contradict* what I have just been saying—that the loss of our original sensual, animal, and wild natures is irrevocable!

Since, according to the wisdom-steam to which I belong, we are embedded in soul at all times, no matter what stage of the consciousness-world constitution we are "in", then we need to look more closely at the nature of such transformations as they occur through history. The objective soul undergoes transformations through time, yes. And these transformations result in irrevocable losses that we humans suffer. For example, the bloody French Revolution, when seen as a soul phenomenon, reveals that the soul movement, within the various empirical motives, ambitions, revenge of people, has to do with a self-overcoming of a soul quality that the soul itself had held in highest esteem for countless centuries and millennia—the majesty of *Being*! In the same way, the soul has overcome its own valued qualities as reflected in natural nature—its life, its vitality, its animal wisdom, its sensual reality, it's luminosity (intelligence, consciousness) and numinosity (power to strike its message home into the receptive human heart) etc. But, in being soul, these self-transformations are always *soul-internal* self-transformations and thus nothing is, after all, lost—this being the axiom by which my entire argument proceeds. [2] A transformation is a *form* change and "something" must endure through that transformation as well as there being a complete going-under, otherwise it would not be a transformation but only a substitution.[3] We are forced to think this contradiction when considering transformations within soul and this is where Hegel's *aufheben* becomes so vital. Everything lost, irrevocable, dead to us forever, yes! Nothing lost, everything prior appearing at a new level of consciousness-world constitution in the very form of that consciousness, equally, yes!

Sublation!

This book is thus a sustained exploration of sublation, as occurring now in the 21st C. as we appear to be suffering yet another self-transformation in our consciousness-world constitution. We appear to be in a soul process of overcoming solidity and entering a new consciousness-world constitution in which the animal, the sensual, the wild, are indeed

---

[2]   See Mogenson's clarifying essay, *Interiorizing Psychology into Itself* in (Giegerich, Miller, & Mogenson, 2005). Particularly see pp. 68-72.

[3]   Owen Barfield explores this point in great detail. See (Barfield O., 1965, p. 104ff).

returning, but at a totally new and unheard-of level of complexity of consciousness.

There is also a new art form appearing that is (as art had been for so long) the *avant-garde* of this incredible appearance amongst us: an "appearance" that Jung calls the *Coming Guest* and what I call, the *twice-born*! [4] I describe several examples of this "art", more correctly called "poesis", emerging through human experiences today, which seem to offer hints of the nature of this "appearance" amongst us. I am thus claiming that natural nature is, after all, not lost, appearing now as the very form of consciousness that is superseding the current soul-world constitution (our world of solidity).

---

[4]   Letter to Sir Herbert Read (Jung, 1975, p. 591).

THE PROBLEM AND ITS
PHILOSPHICAL BACKGROUND

Owen Barfield's life spanned the 20th C. and almost all of his professional work was dedicated to explicating one thought: the evolution of consciousness. That this work of a lifetime was much more than an academic exercise can be seen in his book, *Unancestral Voice*, in which a series of dialogues occur between the author (as Burgeon) and a spiritual being by the name of the *Meggid*. [5] The substance of these conversations concerns the plight of the modern individual now living in a world that is, as far as our ordinary experience of the senses goes, completely bereft of spirit, or intrinsic meaning. Speaking as one of his characters, Chevalier, Barfield considers our current crisis: "How long will it last? Perhaps history *can* give us a line on that . . . . [Burgeon] has taken me back a thousand years [to the historical moment when the Catholic Church eliminated the connection between the human soul and spirit]. I will give him another thousand" to which, in response, Burgeon muses "I don't know. But I rather think things have begun to move faster than that. Perhaps it is [our] fate in the next *hundred years* that we should really be thinking of." [6]

The wide-spread anticipation of an *imminent* crisis that carries the gravest threat to us all now finds expression in so many ways today that I do not intend here to reiterate any of the countless variations that can easily be found

---

[5]   (Barfield O., 1965)

[6]   Ibid: p. 103

across disciplines, in the arts, or in popular media. Instead I want to focus on one particular *formulation* of the crisis that is increasingly gaining attention as perhaps the *central* formulation, from which all other descriptions of the crisis seem to follow (e.g. ecological, economic, ethical, demographical, meteorological, etc.) I am speaking of the *philosophical/psychological* formulation of our crisis in terms of a separation, an unbridgeable gulf, or a Great Divide between our human consciousness and the world. Even within *this* generally agreed-upon formulation, there are still more variations of description that are readily available. [7] In simple terms we can express it this way:

We exist today as conscious on-lookers, looking on a world that is comprised of solid objects in space that, in themselves, do not have consciousness or, *"Nature has a "material, self-external existence, which can never be thought or explained away".* [8]

This of course is the world bequeathed to us by science, over time, as a methodological stance slowly became a collective habit of thought. We can immediately read some startling and provocative implications in this claim I just made: a collective habit of thought sinks into unconsciousness and re-appears as the perceived world! And, prior to science's arrival on the scene, there was no such collective habit of thought and therefore reality was not so constituted as on-lookers gazing upon a collection of solid objects in space!

It cannot be my purpose here to do a review of the relevant literature that advocates these views and indeed counts these

---

[7]   My doctoral program's Bibliography provides for a small sample from the vast literature that explores this subject, available at *www.lighthousedownunder.com*.

[8]   (Harris, 1993, p. 10) quoted in (Foldes, 2013), endnote [2].

views as *knowledge*. That review is properly placed in my doctoral program and, as such, stands as a testimony to the time and effort required to comprehend these implications as well as the wisdom gained over centuries that leads to them—not to mention the post-doctoral research that has followed! [9] Suffice it to say here that the stream of wisdom that underpins everything I have to say here teaches that consciousness and world are correlative, and evolution must therefore mean that as soon as one changes then the other has also changed. Our modern constitution of reality can be shown to have evolved from that of former times, which were constituted radically differently from ours. Thus our times and our reality are not absolute. [10]

The ordinary modern mind today, as well as other philosophical points of view, utterly rejects this stream of wisdom, claiming instead that our modern reality is the only one that has ever been and will always be. Any investigation of nature (such as the one I am doing here) that is therefore not empirically based is not wisdom but instead "comprise[s] only a tissue of fantastic imaginings". [11] This stance dominates today but, nonetheless, having declared my allegiance to the axioms of the wisdom-stream stated above, I can move forward to introduce the flurry of interest that currently springs from an *impulse* emerging from our current world-wide crisis, so understood in its philosophical/ psychological formulation. This impulse is being expressed in many ways but simply put, it says:

---

[9]   My doctoral thesis is available online at *www.lighthousedownunder.com.*
[10] A succinct, clear description of these transformations can be found in Wolfgang Giegerich's essay *The Historicity of Myth* found in (Giegerich, Miller, & Mogenson, 2005, p. 41).
[11] (Stone, 2013)

How can we overcome it? That is how can we overcome the world as it is currently constituted—an on-looking self-consciousness correlative with solid objects placed in empty space? Or, in short, how can we overcome solidity?

To give just some representative examples of variations of this very strange question from within the stream of wisdom to which I am dedicated, I can begin with Vladimir Solovyov (1853-1900). First, he describes our ordinary material existence as a two-fold impenetrability: [12]

Impenetrability in time, by the power of which each successive moment of existence does not preserve the preceding one within itself . . .

And

Impenetrability in space, by power of which two parts of matter (two bodies) cannot at the same time occupy one and the same place . . .

Solovyov then speaks of the task of overcoming this "two-fold impenetrability".

This "overcoming" of solidity, according to Solovyov begins with the *a priori* that "the body of the universe is the totality of the real-ideal" and so the task is to "make the real external medium conformable to the inner unity-of-the-all idea", a task that is "as simple in general conception as it is complex and difficult in concrete realization". [13]

Even Solovyov's general conception is difficult for the modern mind to grasp but it can be made clearer by a

---

[12]   (Solovyov, 1985)

[13]   Ibid: pp. 106-108

comparison with that of Hegel. In Alison Stone's essay, *Hegel's Philosophy of Nature: Overcoming the Division Between Matter and Thought*, the author offers a succinct, accessible description and defense of Hegel's philosophy of nature, beginning with the *a priori* that "reality is self-developing rational thought". [14] It does at first seem question-begging to show how the task of overcoming solidity (or, as she formulates it—overcoming the division between matter and thought) is already accomplished in the first place. This is precisely what is denied by the modern mind—that there is any such connection between the world of nature and modern consciousness, in its status as on-looker. But she later goes on to carefully explain Hegel's thought which shows how modern consciousness emerges from metaphysics, a status of soul which is still "embroiled" in materiality, or reflecting itself in materiality. When this soul thinks of materiality as external to itself, it simultaneously redefines itself as consciousness, now separate from this materiality: [15]

What becomes clear from these two examples is that, in order even to begin to think the possibility of overcoming solidity (the gulf between consciousness and external world), as a way to address our modern crisis, we must start with its already being overcome—externality *is* the expelled corporality, sensations, and emotions of (what once was) the metaphysical soul.

Stone goes on to explain this contradiction in terms of a failure by the ego to recognize itself as a "generator of conceptions of objects" and instead simply sees objects as something passively encountered. [16]

---

[14]   (Stone, 2013)
[15]   Ibid
[16]   Ibid

Owen Barfield describes the stream of wisdom to which Solovyov and Hegel belong this way: [17]

Originality takes us forward, not because it thinks what was never thought before, but because it thinks in harmony with the 'origin' of its subject matter. [Authors like Solovyov and Hegel—my insert] *are timely and fruitful blossoms on a tree, whose roots are deep in the past . . . . The tree is perhaps as old as Yggdrasil itself . . .* [Other blossoms include] *Pythagoras—Platonism—Sufism—Dante—the Fedili d'Amore of Renaissance—the Rosa Alchemica—the Rosicrucian impulse—Hermeticism—Romanticism.*

Barfield further proposes that this wisdom-stream has not remained the same throughout the centuries but has developed! Its earlier manifestations concentrated on the vertical dimension (man-God) with a later emphasis on the horizontal dimension (man-world), as expressed above by Solovyov and Hegel, in the sense that they are both concerned with the unity *within* the diverse solid, impenetrable, objects of the world. [18]

The sentiment infusing this effort of overcoming solidity (as I will now succinctly put it) thus runs very deep historically and has now gained a quality of urgency, leading to a renewed interest in the works of Solovyov and Hegel, for example, as offering guidance for a "way out" of our crisis which is one characterized by four essential features: meaninglessness, loss of our former embeddedness in nature (alienation), ontological homelessness, and, as empirical individual beings, frightening, or even horrifying, dispensability. Our art, literature, economic and political systems, degradation of the environment, medical and psychological findings,

---

[17]   (Solovyov, 1985) from the Introduction by Owen Barfield.

[18]   Ibid

and popular media, shout this at us on a daily basis, and we cannot stand what we are hearing!

An example of the (perhaps too hopeful and sunny) enthusiasm with which Hegel is being embraced by some who sense the urgency and imminence of our crisis in modern life can be found in passages such as this: [19]

Ken Foldes is author, lecturer, and Fulbright Scholar and currently working on his new book The Meaning of The Present Age: Hegel, God, and Foundation. He is convinced we stand on the brink of a glorious new era of world history, made possible by Hegel's achievement of absolute knowing and Wissenschaft.

We have so far found our way to a philosophical/ psychological formulation of the crisis that seems explanatory of these dire characteristics marking our age but we do not want to stay there in this crisis. We want out, as can be felt in the above quote! How *can* we, like Solovyov, and so many others aspire to, overcome this world as constituted today, restoring, so it is hoped, a connection with nature, and with one another, thereby countering the dreadful degradation of both nature and individuals today? It's one thing to point the way via these great individuals but, with the pressing urgency of modern existence today, can this "pointing" lead to an experience that counts!

What kind of experience would comprise a real overcoming of solidity today—the kind of overcoming that this wisdom-stream is pointing us to? And what kind of conditions must prevail for this experience to happen? Is it even possible, in actuality?

---

[19]   Author description by *GWF Hegel.org* in Foldes' essay op. cit.

The first distinction I want to make at this point may be put this way: can solidity (or the present consciousness-world constitution) overcome itself and/or can individuals have an experience in which solidity is really overcome even though such experience occurs within our time, the time of solidity! As we will see these two aspects of the issue are closely related.

These formulations of overcoming solidity only make sense if they and the "problem" are located within the venerable wisdom-stream that I have outlined here and which places the evolution of consciousness at its centre. Consciousness and world are understood as correlative and the transformation of the one means that the other has already transformed too. I will sometimes be referring to overcoming solidity as overcoming our consciousness-world constitution to emphasize the correlative nature of consciousness and world.

This is what we will turn to next.

EVOLUTION OF CONSCIOUSNESS

In his famous essay, *The Abolition of Man*, C. S. Lewis forcefully and cogently argues towards the inevitable conclusion of what he calls "Man's conquest of Nature". Nature, according to Lewis has become, "the world of quantity, as against the world of quality; of objects as against consciousness; of the bound, as against the wholly or partially autonomous . . ." and therefore is manipulable by "Man" through acts of "Power". He goes further in describing nature before it became the world of solid objects, without spirit: [20]

We do not look at trees either as Dryads or as beautiful objects while we cut them into beams: the first man who did so may have felt the price keenly, and the bleeding trees in Virgil and Spenser may be far-off echoes of that primeval sense of impiety. The stars lost their divinity as astronomy developed, and the Dying God has no place in chemical agriculture. To many, no doubt, this process is simply the gradual discovery that the real world is different from what we expected, and the old opposition to Galileo or to `body-snatchers' is simply obscurantism. But that is not the whole story. It is not the greatest of modern scientists who feel most sure that the object, stripped of its qualitative properties and reduced to mere quantity, is wholly real. Little scientists, and little unscientific followers of science, may think so. The great minds know very well that the object, so treated, is an artificial abstraction, that something of its reality has been lost.

---

[20]   (Lewis, C. S., 2013).

The inevitable conclusion is, according to Lewis, as the title suggests, that human beings will be reduced to artifacts, or raw material to be manipulated by a minority called "the Conditioners" who are themselves at the mercy of their sheer animal appetites and therefore sub-human, "vexed no longer by its [Man's] chatter of truth and mercy and beauty and happiness".

Owen Barfield is generous in his praise of Lewis' "iron logic" in this essay, a logic that is "authentically analytical for almost the first time since the decline of Scholasticism", "because it is free from secret physical presuppositions". [21] This essay, as well as other writings of C. S. Lewis, reveals a definitive stance in Lewis' view of the spiritual life that draws Barfield's sympathetic appraisal (in terms of its non-physical presuppositions): [22]

The spiritual life of man, too, consists just a succession of choices—choices that are mutually and absolutely exclusive. In no sense is the spiritual life ever to be thought of as a flow, or a development. It is a series of steps, and each separate step is either in the direction of heaven or it is in the direction of hell.

Lewis' underlying stance on the spiritual life is shared throughout the community of those seeking to somehow overcome solidity and bring our alienation from nature to an end as well as restore a "sacred connection' with nature. Lewis' essay clearly shows his view that our crisis today stems from "a succession of choices" made by human beings that are leading us to hell. It also shows how Lewis and indeed many others in the field believe that the reality of nature as experienced by our forbears (the divinity of the

---

[21]   (Barfield, O., 1989, p.84).

[22]   Ibid.

stars, the dryadic reality of trees, etc.) is still available to us but for the fact that we humans have turned away from it, through our manipulations of nature by the willful exercise of the scientific mind. It is not hard to see lurking within this widely shared stance, epitomized by the Christian Lewis, a view of history as the Downfall. Our modern crisis is the result of choices we humans make—choices that so far are leading us away from heaven into the hell of "the Conditioners"! And, of course, the Christian diagnosis of our modern day crisis leads to a typically Christian solution: hope for a general repentance and regeneration: [23]

The regenerate science which I have in mind would not do even to minerals and vegetables what modern science threatens to do to man himself. When it explained it would not explain away. When it spoke of the parts it would remember the whole. While studying the It it would not lose what Martin Buber calls the Thou-situation . . . . In a word, it would conquer Nature without being at the same time conquered by her and buy knowledge at a lower cost than that of life.

It's clear from this passage that Lewis puts the blame entirely on us human beings for choosing to exalt and privilege analytical thinking, thereby willfully "conquering nature" and reducing the 'thou' to an 'it'. We did it. It is our fault—a fault that may, hopefully, be corrected if we start to make different choices.

Within proponents of overcoming solidity (keeping in mind that this is my shorthand for overcoming our currently constituted reality of a gulf between consciousness and a world of solid objects), Lewis perhaps stands as an exemplar. For this reason, a more penetrating look into his *background* system of thought may bring to light how he, and others,

---

[23]   (Lewis, C. S., 2013)

could come to this conclusion that our modern crisis is only the result of a "succession of human choices" etc.

The life-long friendship between C. S. Lewis and Owen Barfield included vigorous and mutually benefitting conversations on the nature of the imagination. Barfield is perhaps uniquely qualified to give us insight into, not only the conscious content of Lewis' thinking, but also the background structure of Lewis' mind that gave rise to the content in the first place. In *Lewis, Truth and Imagination*, Barfield refers to the "logical Lewis" and the "imaginative Lewis" as well as to the gulf between them. [24] He tells us how Lewis' logical mind could expose "muddleheaded" positions that are still so popular today. For example, he shows how Lewis successfully attacks the tendency to reduce all spiritual concerns to the physical (materialism), "by way of a battery of very simple, very lucid, and totally unanswerable arguments reinforced by equally simple and vigorous metaphors". [25]

But the one area for Lewis that remained off-limits to such penetrating analysis was the imagination. Instead, Lewis' relation to imagination was one of love, a very particular form of love: [26]

[Lewis] was in love with it. And being in love (which is not quite coterminous with "having sex") has been observed to entail a strong impulse to protect the beloved object from contamination, a kind of horror at the contrast between her perfections and the harsh world of reality . . . . It was the Victorians who gave fullest expression to this not altogether ignoble impulse. When it became apparent that there was not much prospect of making the world nobler, at all events in the

---

[24]   (Barfield O., 1989, p. 94)

[25]   Ibid: p. 91

[26]   Ibid: p. 98

immediate future, it was felt that the next best thing was to insulate the beloved from it altogether . . . so that it could continue to live its own pure and chaste life; to insulate it, therefore, from having anything to do with fact.

For Lewis, the imagination could therefore have no relation to truth and thus could play no part in the study of history and *its* truths. Barfield also explores Lewis' relation to history in considerable detail. [27] Without going into the complexity of Lewis' stance re: history, as elucidated by Barfield, we can say this much, that Lewis did not accept an evolution of consciousness in the way that Barfield does. Lewis, importantly for the purposes of this essay, also discounted any possibility of the use of the imagination in gaining any *knowledge* of historical times. It appears he had no understanding of, or appreciation of, Coleridge's famous distinction between imagination and fancy in his claim that (as summarized by Barfield): [28] [29]

A historian may think he sees patterns, or a pattern in them [the aggregation of heterogeneous details that constitute the past—my insert], *but we see imaginary patterns (faces in the fire, for example) in anything if we look long enough at it. All such patterns are mere guesswork, because actual knowledge depends on the inferring of particular causes from particular effects . . .*

It is my contention here that we are not only looking into the background structure of Lewis' mind here, but also that structure informing the content of the argument itself that claims that:

---

[27]   Ibid: p. 67ff

[28]   Ibid: p. 68

[29]   (Barfield O., 1978). See chapters, *Imagination and Fancy.*

a) spirit is only eternal such that every generation of human beings is "equidistant from eternity". [30] There is no evolution of consciousness such that history can become expressive of spiritual movement in (as) time;

b) our modern crisis formulated as a consciousness-world split is solely a result of step-by-step human choices that have led us away from the vision of nature as still divine, still alive with spirit and

c) the crisis can be corrected by a series of counter step-by-step choices that can lead back to that particular, preferred vision of nature.

There literally is no other way to account for how we got here to this crisis if from the start we exclude the imagination as an organ of truth (as applied to history) and if we inoculate and exalt one preferred vision of nature (in Lewis' case, the Victorian vision of nature) against, as Barfield argues, *facts* (such as the fact that our "vision of nature" has changed over time). The only account left possible is that we humans have made a series of missteps, which may be corrected if we follow Lewis' and other like-minded people's exhortations. To date (2013) there seems to me not a shred of evidence that this has happened, or will.

Perhaps, therefore, the mind-set that leads to this "blaming of humanity" as the sole cause of the crisis is mistaken! If we do not mindlessly adopt the "Lewis mind-set" (as summarized in the points above), then we are free to re-examine the whole issue of our modern-day crisis and its "causes", as well as deepen our comprehension of what overcoming solidity could possibly mean, if not a series of steps that return us to that particular vision of nature that Lewis (and many others, if we

---

[30]   Op. Cit.: p. 73.

witness the enormous popularity of movies such as *Avatar*) preferred.

In contrast to Lewis, Barfield's life-long work is rooted in his comprehension of the truth of there being an evolution of consciousness, or more exactly, an evolution of the consciousness-world constitution. [31] [32] The vehicle for arriving at this truth is what may be called the historical imagination as applied to the language of historical documents (art, texts etc.) In brief this is a method of looking into the past. He notes the prodigious efforts of scholarship in collating vast amounts of knowledge concerning our past. But, instead of simply thinking about that past, he claims that through a disciplined act of imagination, we can penetrate the language of the past and feel our way into it, bringing that world alive for us as a kind of historical presence. [33]

He gives us one particularly compelling example in his study of how the meaning of the modern word "ruins" i.e., a building or thing that has fallen into disrepair, has evolved from earlier meanings of rushing, or "swift, disastrous movement". [34] Following his method, Barfield begins with a scholarly etymological study of the word, but then moves into the historical imagination as he begins to reconstruct, in his imagination, what constitution of consciousness-world (reality) must have been in place, as expressed in the language of the precursors to the modern word, "ruins".

There was thus a time (as reconstructed in the historical imagination) when sound and meaning were one, as

---

[31] He called this philosophical position: *Objective Idealism*. See (Barfield O., 1963) as expressed through the voice of Sanderson.

[32] See, for example, (Barfield O., 1979).

[33] See chapter, *Philology and The Aryans* in (Barfield O., 1967a).

[34] See (Barfield O., 1973, p. 113 ff) from which the following description of the evolution of consciousness is drawn.

expressed in "the old, guttural, rumbling 'r', which our modern palates have so thinned and refined, [and which] once had its concrete connection with swift, natural movements such as those torrents or landslides." The form of consciousness-world here is one of maximum participation and minimum self-consciousness—one in which the world speaks through the human being who has not yet distinguished himself from it. We might say all consciousness (inwardness, interiority) is over on the side of the world. A modern example of this reality can be found in the traditional didgeridoo of Australian aboriginals. What one hears through the instrument is nature—birds, storms, whales, etc., but not discretely so, in the way that these modern nouns *now* convey. It is not a man imitating these sounds; it is nature sounding itself through the instrument in its original cacophony. There is no signature to the "music". We are not yet hearing man's interpretation of nature. In the didgeridoo we are probably hearing language itself coming into being, and along with it, humankind's emergence from total embeddedness in nature, *as* humans (i.e. linguistic).

Barfield next moves etymologically from the sound-meaning 'r' to 'ruo', the Latin verb which still carries a lively sense of movement but now conveys, in addition to rushing, a distinguishable sense of falling, collapsing. The historical imagination now suggests that this word came to convey a "conscious realization by men that such motions, with the noise that accompanies them, are often the prelude to disaster . . ." We are now reconstructing a reality in which human beings have gained inwardness or interiority, and the world has gained hitherto unknown contours (rushing quality as distinct from falling, collapsing), although fluidity still dominates the qualities of this world. The word, "rua" gives rise to "ruina" which is substantive, conveying a reference not only to a movement of falling, but also to "the thing fallen". Now the historical imagination informs us that the contours of the world are hardening, standing out in sharp relief, "arrested", more solid, while self-consciousness is, in turn, more and more looking on, no longer participating in the object. Barfield says of this historical process, "it is like watching a physical process of crystallization", (i.e., to the historical imagination).

He gives us another example that forcefully drives home how consciousness and world are always correlative in their mutual transformation through time. In his book *Saving the Appearances*, which lays out his central ideas regarding the evolution of consciousness (and world), he first demonstrates the easy case of the real rainbow necessarily involving the participation of human consciousness in its undeniable "realness". Without human participation, the rainbow is simply the "unrepresented particles" of physics. Then, he offers a quite startling example that challenges whether we really do believe what we in fact easily accept regarding the nature of the real rainbow. On exactly the same reasoning, we must accept that the realness of solid things *also* depends on our participation with the thing.

Solidity is not a reality independent of consciousness! [35]

We can see from these examples that our current world of solidity can be understood as the end point (so far) of a long process of evolution of the consciousness-world constitution. Barfield shows throughout his works that human beings' self-consciousness increasingly comes into prominence in this process with new contours of the world being perceived (coming into being) as new meaning is poured into familiar words. [36] We can further see that Lewis' ahistoricism (see

---

[35] (Barfield O., 1957, p. 22ff)
[36] See (Barfield O., 1967b) and *Poetic Diction and Legal Fiction* in (Barfield O., 1977).

point "a" above) completely occludes the evolution of consciousness from consideration in the vexed question of overcoming solidity.

The evolution of consciousness (very briefly) thus describes a consciousness-world constitution that transforms over time, with consciousness becoming more and more an on-looking self-consciousness and world becoming more and more "crystallized", as Barfield puts it. Now we are in a position to ask if this process could solely be the result of human beings making step-by-step choices, as Lewis would have it.

Barfield's life-long study of simile, metaphor, and symbolism demonstrates how, with increasing self-consciousness, human beings could actively "create" (i.e. draw out of potentiality into actuality) new aspects of world, or as I put it, fresh contours of the world. [37] [38] This creative process however, is not idiosyncratic, not personality-based. I explore the deeper, more complex aspects of this creative process of the changing consciousness-world constitution in my own book but suffice it to say here that Barfield understands fully that there is a "spiritual background" working its determinations through the human being down through history! [39] [40] This understanding cannot possibly be available to C. S. Lewis and those proponents of spirit "outside time" who therefore are forced to account for our current crisis on the theological basis of, "All good lies with God, all bad lies with Man"!

Barfield formalizes his comprehension of the evolution of consciousness in terms of a crucial distinction within historical research: the history of ideas and the history of

---

[37]   (Barfield O., 1977, p. 50 ff)
[38]   (Barfield O., 1973, p. 112)
[39]   (Woodcock J. C., 2012c)
[40]   See in particular, (Barfield O., 1965).

consciousness. [41] The history of ideas may be thought of as a "dialogue between contemporaries". [42] Ultimately this view of history assumes that different philosophers (for example) are confronted with the same world (*our* modern world of solid objects in space etc.) and generate similar ideas about that world, ideas that improve over time. However, this assumption cannot be so when we are studying the history of consciousness. Given that the world of real appearances depends in part at least on the participation of human beings (what Barfield calls figuration and thinking), then a study of consciousness over time is necessarily also a study of changes in the world of real appearances. [43] [44]

C. S. Lewis does, however, make an important contribution to the theory of history in his claim that history is "the belief that men can, by the use of their natural powers, discover an inner meaning in the historical process". He regards history as an "aggregation of heterogeneous details" (i.e., in themselves meaningless) and, though the historian may think he sees a pattern, this is no more meaningful than gazing into a fire. Barfield disputes this characterization by reminding us of Coleridge's distinction between imagination and fancy, as well as developments that have taken place within hermeneutics. [45]

However, Lewis' characterization of the past as in itself comprising a meaningless aggregation is very close to Herder's understanding of history, given at the time when we were collectively awakening to history *as* history, i.e., as a discipline.

---

[41]   (Barfield O., 1979)

[42]   Ibid: p. 8

[43]   (Barfield O., 1957, p. 22ff)

[44]   (Barfield O., 1979, p. 18)

[45]   (Barfield O., 1989, pp. 68-69)

Herder posits the past primarily as a rubble heap of isolated facts, a collection of details from all ages, from all parts of the world, having no intrinsic meaning but simply awaiting organization by the historian who can make visible the spirit which breathes in everything. The historian can now contemplate history, which makes no demands on him, no claims. [46] Lewis and Herder did not seem to comprehend that the idea of past as a meaningless rubble, making no binding claims on humans is not a given. It was *posited* as such by Herder, opening up a gulf between observer and historical fact, and rendering history harmless. History, however, was once the Present or nothing at all. History as "the ancestors" was a living reality and, when it appeared it did so as an advent. We cannot say "the ancestors" were yet a *psychological* reality because psychology, like history, came along much later. But the ancestors did impose a living claim on human beings at a time when Meaning reigned, when it was bestowed on human beings and had its own authority/power within itself. It was self-evident, requiring no human interpretation (hermeneutics). In this sense, history was initiatory. The essence of the human being was transformed though the encounter, unreflectingly.

A modern example of this ancient sense of history may be found in a biography of an American Indian shaman, who describes his initiatory vision this way: [47]

When we had camped again, I was lying in our tepee and my mother and father were sitting beside me. I could see out through the opening, and there two men were coming from the clouds, headfirst like arrows slanting down, and I knew they were the same I had seen before. Each now carried a long

---

[46]   In the following discussion of psychological history I am indebted to Wolfgang Giegerich. See *The Alchemy of History* in (Giegerich W., 2008).

[47]   (Neihardt, 2008). See Chapter 3: *The Great Vision.*

spear, and from the points of these a jagged lightning flashed. They came clear down to the ground this time and stood a little way off and looked at me and said, "Hurry! Come! Your Grandfathers are calling you! . . . Your Grandfathers all over the world are having a council, and have called you here to teach you". His voice was very kind but I shook all over with fear, for I knew these were not old men but Powers of the world.

The transformation in the meaning of history is an important consideration in the issue of "overcoming solidity" because, as both Barfield and Giegerich point out, we can today have a thorough understanding of historical development (such as the evolution of consciousness) and yet remain remarkably untouched in our consciousness by any of it, quite in contrast to Black Elk's experience of the ancestors. For example, Giegerich, moving along the same lines of Lewis in his assessment of the effects of the scientific mind on the divinity of nature (see Lewis quote above, p. 9) says of the task of science: [48]

Their true task had been to remove from the events their ontologically startling, penetrating nature, to neutralize or paralyse them ontologically and in this way to render man essentially immune to whatever can still happen to him as before [i.e., empirically—my insert].

Barfield also fully recognizes our immunity to penetration from the *other* in his concept of unresolved positivism. [49]

Nowhere have I found any real grasp of this central fact: that self-consciousness, that subjectivity itself, is an historical process. There are hints of it perhaps in Jung; and sometimes some of the anthropologists—Durkheim, for example, or

---

[48]   (Giegerich W., 2008, p. 369).
[49]   (Barfield O., 1966, p. 190)

Levy-Bruhl, with his 'participation mystique'—seem to imply it. But sooner or later they drop some remark which shows that at the bottom of their imaginations they still believe that man has always, in fact, been what the Phenomenologists would call 'an embodied self in Nature'—neither more nor less of a self than he is today. They show that they do not really believe that man's consciousness ever was a part of nature's any more than it is now. But only that he made a mistake and thought it was-a very different thing.

We might say that both authors here are pointing to the intractable problem of overcoming solidity in actual experience. We may have the *knowledge* of the evolution of consciousness or of the urgent need to overcome the gulf between self and nature but remain ineluctably immune to any of that knowledge penetrating to our core and transforming our consciousness-world constitution. [50] Or to put it another way, the past, although it can be remembered, or even empathized with, remains on the other side of a gulf, so that the consciousness of the past is no longer available to us, as an initiatory force, penetrating our modern consciousness and transforming it. [51]

For the historian, the rift valley stands between him and what he studies. Even if he studies the most recent events in the past, they are nevertheless, by definition, construed as events in the past, nothing but the past. The historian may, to be sure, imagine *and empathize himself into former ages, but these times do not, from a methodological point of view, become for him a present that is seen from within . . . He merely switches sides, leaving the Great Divide out there between himself and the event . . .*

---

[50] I. e., overcoming solidity in actual experience, whatever that could mean! The purpose of my essay here is to explore this very question.

[51] (Giegerich W., 2008, p. 186)

In other words, we can, as historians or hermeneutic researchers, study the past (e. g., the evolution of consciousness), holding it up as a picture, or imagination, "Beyond all limits of his own time he looks out into the past cultures; he absorbs their strength into himself and re-enjoys his charm; a great increase of happiness arises for him from this." [52] but the events themselves remain, as Lewis tells us, an mere aggregation of [dead] facts, no longer living as realities that could penetrate and initiate the human being. To put it bluntly, we may know all about the evolution of consciousness and of our place in it as modern individuals looking onto a world of solid objects, but that historical knowledge remains as interesting but dead knowledge, of no psychological significance in the sense that the consciousness of the past as thought about by modern consciousness remains in the past, out of reach, dead!

With our modern structure of consciousness, which is highly reflective and interpretive, events cannot psychologically reach us immediately as they once could when original participation prevailed and human beings were simply templates upon which soul reality *could* imprint itself (primarily during that period of time known as the shamanic or ritualistic time). Our modern consciousness, as I have stressed throughout, is separated from the world of events by a gulf. We are on-lookers! Although empirical events may indeed strike us and strike us hard, they remain psychologically external to us and historical events, although objects of "blissful contemplation", no longer strike into our hearts, initiating our consciousness with the kind of binding claim that Black Elk felt.

---

[52]   Wilhelm Dilthey as translated by Wolfgang Giegerich (Giegerich W., 2008, p. 362).

Robert Graves gives another striking example of a *past* consciousness-world constitution in which a human being could both be struck by a real external event *and* bound by its intrinsic meaning—a meaning that carries its own authority and force: [53]

It was in the hands of a magically-minded priesthood, whose duty was to suggest what action would please the gods on peculiarly auspicious or inauspicious occasions. When, for example, a bottomless chasm suddenly opened in the Roman Forum, they read it as a sign that the gods demanded a sacrifice of Rome's best; one Mettus Curtius felt called upon to save the situation by choosing the right thing, and leaped into the chasm on horseback, fully armed.

Today, however, as we have been discussing here, the evolution of consciousness has resulted in self-consciousness, facing a world now bereft in meaning and binding power altogether. As Giegerich puts it: [54]

The real cannot touch and move us; that which touches and moves us has no validity and binding force for the actual Present. Binding force and emotionally touching meaning now belong to separate spheres of authority, namely to [natural sciences] *and to history: a dissociation of the original happening of events . . .*

By "happening", Giegerich is referring to "the occurrence of the *authoritatively* real [amounting to] the primordial unity of natural phenomena and intellectual meaning . . ." which left the nature of Man, as happened with Black Elk and Mettus Curtius, "inescapably exposed to the reigning power of Being". Referring to the consciousness of modern

---

[53]   (Graves, 1994, p. 478)
[54]   (Giegerich W., 2008, pp. 370-371)

human beings as being redeemed from the course of events to a free, "higher" humaneness, Giegerich inquires into the question of what kind of experience is required for us, in our modern state of reflective (redeemed) consciousness to once again come to know of an *other* existing "outside" ourselves, an *other* that autonomously gazes into our existence and has something to say to us of its own accord, thus requiring us to listen mutely, to be written upon. [55]

According to the evolution of consciousness, this *other* can no longer be outside in nature, as it was once in our distant past, or as Black Elk and Mettus Curtius must have experienced: "The individual objects of the world, earth, heaven, springs and fire, sun and moon, wind and mountains have all become hollow of meaning and banal". [56] It is not the case, as Lewis thought, that human beings have willfully turned away from divine nature through a series of missteps or choices. Real objective *otherness* has withdrawn from nature and now can only be found as our inwardness, as the *other* within. [57]

So, if we are indeed in a time of another transformation in the evolution of consciousness, then we can expect to find hints of that transformation in two forms, as I said earlier in my chapter on the problem and its philosophical background. The form of individual experiences of "overcoming solidity" occurs "within" the subject but has the phenomenology of an *other* "breaking in" through our customary immunity (with more or less psychological "violence") and transforming the consciousness-world constitution "within" that individual (i.e., at the depths of that individual's inwardness or interiority). This experience can have the consequence that

---

[55]   Ibid: p. 389-391
[56]   (Giegerich W., 2008, pp. 408-409)
[57]   Barfield offers an excellent description of this transformation of "inwardness" in his essay *Imagination and Inspiration*, found in (Barfield O., 1977).

the individual gains new perceptions corresponding to a new real world. However, such perceptions are only private representations (in Owen Barfield's meaning of that term) and not yet collective representations. [58] This can be quite disconcerting for such an individual. It is tantamount to having to living in two worlds that are colliding. [59]

The second possible form of overcoming solidity is the *objective* form of the world's self-overcoming of solidity, according to the determinations of the evolution of consciousness. [60]

We will turn to the first form next.

---

[58]   For a discussion of this distinction, see (Barfield O., 1957, p. 19 ff).

[59]   See my Chapter below, *Worlds in Collision.*

[60]   Throughout this book I use the word *other*, in italics, or *otherness*: e. g. the *other* within. I do not mean by this a substantive or an entity existing positivistically in us or in space. I mean to make a distinction between contents of consciousness and the "background" logical structure that gives rise to those contents.

INDIVIDUAL EXPERIENCE
OF OVERCOMING SOLIDITY

As I discussed above, if we accept that there is a real movement through history known as the evolution of consciousness, then those efforts to address our current crisis by thinking of it as a result of missteps by human kind, leading us to disaster and requiring reparative steps to restore a pristine world such as C. S. Lewis' nostalgic portrayal, are hopelessly mistaken and misguided. The evolution of consciousness shows a process through time in which the consciousness-world constitution undergoes transformation *and takes us with it.* This is not a human choice! We humans apprehend what has happened to us, under the impact of history, always too late. It has already happened and the philosophical task is simply to make what has happened to us explicit, to make the reality we have been living all along our truth. As Hegel famously says in the Preface to his *Philosophy of Right*:

[P]hilosophy at least always comes too late. Philosophy, as the thought of the world, does not appear until reality has completed its formative process, and made itself ready. History thus corroborates the teaching of the conception that only in the maturity of reality does the ideal appear as counterpart to the real, apprehends the real world in its substance, and shapes it into an intellectual kingdom. When philosophy paints its grey in grey, one form of life has become old, and by means of grey it cannot be rejuvenated, but only known. The owl of Minerva, takes its flight only when the shades of night are gathering.

We seem to be vigorously engaging in a similar process today, in the many modern philosophical descriptions of *our* reality, (called Positivism, Materialism, Reductionism, etc.) which also indicates that another transformation (which I am calling "overcoming solidity") has occurred and is catching up individuals in its processes. Earlier I spoke of the possible phenomenology of such experiences for those individuals so "caught" in the soul's processes of transformation:

We can expect to find any such hints of that transformation only in the form of individual experiences of "overcoming solidity" as occurring within the subject but having the phenomenology of an other *"breaking in" through our customary immunity (with more or less psychological "violence") and transforming the consciousness-world constitution "within" that individual (i.e., in the depths of that individual's inwardness or interiority).*

I now want to give a feel for this complex process by telling some stories that seem to have this question implicitly in mind. Certain traditional fairy tales can shed some light on what kind of experience may involve overcoming solidity in the context of our modern reality. As well as these I will present a modern fairy tale that is expressive of the author's conscious attempt to lay down the psychological conditions that need to prevail for an actual experience of overcoming solidity. I will then turn to some biographical accounts of what appears to me to be actual instances of an individual's undergoing an actual initiation into a new reality. These accounts give us a hint of how a transformation of the current consciousness-world constitution is now being experienced by individuals. Finally I want to offer further evidence that the transformation has already happened and that we no longer psychologically live in a world of solidity but instead, in our essence, are already well beyond any substantiality at all. We live, in our essence, in a consciousness-world constitution that may be called pure movement (mediality).

First two traditional fairy tales: [61]

In a local legend from Alcace, the father of St. Odelia wants to force her to marry a certain man. She runs away and kneels in front of a wall of rock in order to pray. The rock opens, enclosing her and lets her out only after her father has given up his plan to marry her to that man.

In a local legend from Corinthia a poor farm worker who because of his poverty cannot marry his bride runs with his forehead against a grey stone half the size of a man. Now he notices a small door in the wall of a rock, goes into a gallery and comes into a large hall shiny with gold and silver. A beautiful woman fills his pockets with rocks, leads him to an armchair out of silver where he falls asleep. When he awakens, he is outside, and there is no door in the rock any more.

We can see within the narrative structure of these stories an implicit idea of "overcoming solidity". They both invoke impossibility: a rock opening up and enclosing the heroine or a small doorway opening up to a large hall. The sense of another dimension being involved is hinted at by the sleep-awake motif in the second story. Fairy tales and myths are faint echoes of a *reality* that, according to the evolution of consciousness, we have left far behind. However, we can approach this reality through the text of the stories, as Barfield has shown, in such a way that the *consciousness* of this past may once again become available to us. If we do this, we can begin to sense that we are being shown how the soul or Mind

---

[61] These tales and the discussion that follows are drawn from Wolfgang Giegerich's essay, *The Leap into The Solid Stone*: (Giegerich W., 2010).

is working out for itself the *dynamics* of overcoming solidity. In order to enter and participate in this consciousness, we must begin with the *a priori* that there is no external referent in the story; everything is a property of the Mind including solidity. We are not here talking about a mind that is referring to solid things outside it because to do so is to remain within our present state of modern consciousness. To find our way back to this ancient form of consciousness prior to the rupture between self-consciousness and world, the stories must be absolutely inwardized.

Solidity (impenetrable rock) must be, for the Mind, a complete thwarting of the will.

Gaston Bachelard has shown in his beautiful imaginations of earth that it is in the hardness or resistance of matter that we find the exercise of our will. [62] This thought finds resonance with Barfield's understanding of the evolution of consciousness in which the world today, as a finished work (solid matter), as perceived and thought by the modern mind, is correlative to the modern will. [63] The Mind, as shown in the stories, intent on escaping, fleeing, getting out of a situation (marriage, poverty), finds itself only going more deeply into the situation. All attempts to exit only intensify the entrapment. *Willing* a way out intensifies the hardening, in these accounts. There is no breakthrough in the sense that the will accomplishes its intended mission on the same plane of existence as before. There would be no point to the tales if this were the case. We can see instead that a "breakthrough" does occur and this breakthrough is pictured as a *new dimension* opening up—one that was simply not there before.

---

[62]   (Bachelard, 2002)

[63]   (Barfield O., 1966, p. 201 ff).

We can perhaps usefully compare these stories with Dante's picture of the deepest level of Hell which is a region of increasing constriction and cold formed by Satan's fall from Heaven into the bowels of Earth. At the bottom, a topography of maximum constriction, Satan, still longing for Heaven ("runnels of tears"), is trapped in petrifying ice and cold, his powerful wings beating furiously in his vain attempt to escape, but the beating wings only solidify the ice further. This is a colossal image of futility, leading to no breakthrough, nor opening up to a new dimension at all. [64]

In comparing these stories of the Mind's self-movements, we can ask, what does the Mind want to imagine to itself? The new dimension in the fairy tales is the Mind's own interiority or inwardness, Mind *as* inwardness itself, and to picture this it shows an image of utter impenetrability, or externality. Today we could say it is a picture of our world of solidity. This very impenetrability is the door to interiority or, as Dante shows us, equally an endpoint, a "no exit" as the Existentialists would have it. Both alternatives apparently involve the will. The difference in outcome may involve the Mind's commitment or total investment in the exercise of its will. Satan *longs* for the past, longs for Heaven, that state that existed before the fall. As long as the Mind yearns for past states, its Present will appear as ineluctable solidity and a condition of futility will only intensify. This of course relates to our own longing for the past (or restoration), in the way C. S. Lewis does. Dante shows us that such longing only deepens and intensifies that condition that we so earnestly seek to "exit".

In contrast, the two fairy tales show the Mind that is fully committed through the will to escape. There is nothing left behind, no nostalgia. And with this fully engaged will,

---

[64] (Aligheri, 1949)

engaging with the intractable matter at hand, the more will is applied, the more intractable the situation becomes: again, no way out! It seems that the Mind in its self-movements, needs to anchor itself fully and unreservedly (unlike Dante's *Satan*) in both its will to escape and its own posited impossibility of escape (pictured as the rock). This "impossibility" is apparently the *sine qua non* of the Mind's breakthrough from positivity to interiority. The Mind escapes from escaping and so remains faithful to its wholeheartedly committed intent, breaking through finally to its own nature as inwardness.

It seems to me that an eloquent attempt to approach this issue of overcoming solidity may be seen, oddly enough, in another work by C. S. Lewis, this time emerging from the imaginative Lewis, as Barfield describes the one pole of the two Lewis' (the other being the logical Lewis, as I said above, p. 12). Lewis' fairy tale, *The Great Divorce* describes the author's finding himself one day in a grey dismal town that turns out to be Hell. From there he journeys with others to Heaven and undergoes some teachings there. The point of interest for my argument here lies in Lewis' graphic and imaginative description of Heaven (interiority). He describes Heaven as being like earth only much more solid: [65]

It was the light, the grass, the trees that were different; made of some different substance, so much solider than things in our country that men were ghosts by comparison. Moved by a sudden thought, I bent down and tried to pluck a daisy which was growing at my feet. The stalk wouldn't break. I tried to twist it, but it wouldn't twist. I tugged till the sweat stood out on my forehead and I had lost most of the skin off my hands. The little flower was hard, not like wood or even like iron, but like diamond. There was a leaf—a young tender beech-leaf, lying in the grass beside it. I tried to pick the leaf up: my heart almost

---

[65] (Lewis, 2010, p. 21)

cracked with the effort, and I believe I did just raise it. But I had to let it go at once; it was heavier than a sack of coal.

In commenting on this central feature of the story Barfield says: "In *The Great Divorce*, Lewis . . . employs not only material shapes but materiality itself to symbolize immateriality . . . .". [66] He is saying here that Lewis is giving us a picture of the inwardness of solidity, an inwardness that Positivism or Materialism utterly denies. This imaginative picture further suggests that the overcoming of solidity lies somehow within solidity itself, as I have already discussed above. The story also makes it clear that while Lewis was able to present such a picture, and participate in it as a fictional character, the actual experience of overcoming solidity was beyond his reach:

Next moment the folds of my [Heavenly] *Teacher's garment were only the folds of the old ink-stained cloth on my study table which I had pulled down with me as I fell from my chair. The blocks of light were only the books which I had pulled off with it, falling about my head. I awoke in a cold room, hunched on the floor beside a black and empty grate, the clock striking three, and the siren howling overhead.*

The structure of the whole story is that of a narrator telling a dream, from which he wakens to the ordinary world, with everything the same as before. [67]

The following modern autobiographical account is, in my judgment, a description of overcoming solidity, in actuality! [68] A *Newsweek* journalist was captured and tortured over 118

---

[66] (Barfield O., 1989, p. 88)

[67] Op. Cit. PP. 145-146.

[68] I am grateful to Russell Lockhart who reports this episode in *Dreams in the News*: Dream Network Journal, Spring 2010.

days in Iran, 2009. He was thus literally in a situation of "no escape" and was mercilessly beaten. During this torture he reports a "dream" he had in which two women appeared, accompanied by a song by Leonard Cohen, *Sisters of Mercy*: [69]

From that moment Leonard Cohen became the guardian of my universe. He was the secret that Mr. Rosewater [his torturer] *could never discover.*

In cases of extreme trauma, there are well-documented cases of dissociation where the victim "leaves the body" and is thus "outside" the pain that continues being inflicted on their body. They may even perceive themselves being tortured, from "outside". Accident victims, surgery patients, wounded soldiers—all offer instances of this kind of psychological response to trauma. The dissociation, or depersonalization, may become permanent. I believe that Behari's account is pointing to another phenomenon altogether, an overcoming of solidity, along the lines I described earlier. He had discovered what he calls another "universe", populated by figures he could converse with, and apparently he could hear music there, too. This "universe" stayed with him, even subsequent to the dream, and protected him from the harsh treatment, i.e., psychologically. Although he positivizes his experience, i.e., thinks of the figures as people, along with Leonard Cohen, it does seem to me that Behari had found his way into interiority itself, the "new dimension" that lies beyond, and paradoxically within solidity, the concrete impossibility and impenetrability of his empirical situation.

A crucial detail of Behari's experience is that of his having a dream in which two women came to him. It does seem relatively clear, from reading his full account, that this was no ordinary dream. It probably is more accurate to say that

---

[69]   (Behari, 2009)

he had found his way into what he called a "universe", a world which he now inhabited, just like the poor farmer's account of the large hall that opened up for him "through" the impenetrable rock. The portal to this world for Behari was Leonard Cohen's music. Behari could will himself back into that world by singing some lines from Cohen's song, *The Sisters of Mercy,* thus escaping the inescapable, psychologically breaking through into a new dimension—the soul's interiority. In so doing, he overcame solidity in actual experience, although, obviously, his body was still taking dreadful beatings.

This heart-wrenching account, given by a man who managed somehow to stay conscious, with his imagination intact, through such an ordeal, allows us to make some further refinements in our discussion of the individual experience of overcoming solidity. First, to state the obvious, Behari is an eloquent spokesman of solidity as a literal fact, i.e., the hardness and impenetrability of solid things (like fists and belts). Empirically we live inescapably in this world of solid things. This is how the present consciousness-world constitution *is* for us at this time in the evolution of consciousness. And yet, movement of some kind occurred for Behari, movement into a new real dimension where there was none before, where in fact none was possible before, "within" a world comprising only exteriority and hard facts. How can we understand this impossibility more deeply?

We can begin by reframing the question in this way: the evolution of consciousness reveals to us that, with increasing self-consciousness, the world correspondingly lost (what we would call today) its imaginal or symbolic character by which I mean its character as an expression of immaterial reality, or soul. The prime characteristic of today's modern world is one of soullessness, a condition that has produced, as we know through vast literature today, nostalgic calls for a return to sacred nature, or past forms of the consciousness-world constitution, as C. S. Lewis has done throughout his *oeuvre*. In what possible way, then, can our modern world of solid things be symbolic? Movement into imaginal depth or interiority is only possible when outer material reality is symbolic. To give an example of how this works, we can turn to some past forms of consciousness and world, as reconstructed in the mind of modern authors who have a well-developed historical imagination. The example I want to use is taken from the historical novel, *The Coming of the King* by Nicolai Tolstoy. When I read this book, I am taken into that time in which outer reality is expressive of inner reality to a degree that is impossible for us today. For the Celts at that time, it was simply reality. [70]

Merlin and his companion Rufinus, a Roman tribune, are climbing a hill, engaging in animated conversation. As they climb, wild nature begins to encroach and civilized life fades in the distance: [71]

The air was raw and chilly, and cold had arisen upon a wind blowing the full length of the world from the hard unyielding planets set in the void above Dinleu Gurygon . . . A nightjar, twisting silently in the night sky above us, uttered a guttural "churr, churr" from his great gaping mouth . . . From all about me in the heather and upon the rocks came a rustling and squeaking and grunting . . . I heard bats squeaking in the rimy dark and felt faint breeze upon my face from the wings of blundering moths. The cold had become yet more bitter: cold, cold, cold. I felt as if I were frozen into the hard ground, like the exposed outcrop against which I leaned for support. The owl's discordant shriek heralded the rising of a night mist, a vapor from each hollow, an encircling gray hood about the

---

[70]   (Tolstoy, 1989)
[71]   Ibid: p. 254 ff.

hilltop. I did not doubt that it was the mist of Gwyn mab Nud, smoky unguent of the Witches of Annufn, a shaggy mantle over the land . . .

I was wedged in the belly of the hill, my body stiff, cold, and inert. Before me, cross-legged upon a mound, sat a huge skin-clad herdsman, beside him a curly-haired mastiff bigger than a stallion of nine winters. Its breath was such that it would consume dead wood and yellowed tufts of grass upon the open Plain of Powys beneath. In his hand the great swart figure bore an iron club that would be a burden for two men to carry.

Here we can see a seamless transition from ordinary, outer reality to interiority, or soul-life. The outer world is not as hard or impenetrable as ours is today. Outer nature smoothly, as it were, becomes transparent to soul reality, and Merlin finds the mythic Herdsman already there waiting for him. Nature at this stage of the evolution of consciousness nature is still transparent to soul reality. Its reality is still imaginal.

Modern individuals such as Behari have broken through, as we have seen, to soul reality, but it appears, in contrast to the experience of Merlin, to be a much more "violent" process, one that involves contradictions. One such contradiction is that for Behari, the solid world became symbolic, in the way that C. S. Lewis proposes in his essay, *The Great Divorce.* I have so far tried to account for this movement out of non-movement in terms of the will, committedly and unreservedly, willing its way out of a correlative hardness or impenetrability that it (the will) produces in the first place, thereby escaping even escaping, which process, for the mind, produces interiority (the new dimension), i.e., by interiorizing the notion of escape.

The evolution of consciousness teaches us that the time dimension is crucial to our understanding of the transformation in the consciousness-world constitution. This means that there is an irreversibility that we must come to terms with in our considerations of overcoming solidity. Thus, the *way* in which Merlin enters interiority is forever lost to us today. There are no steps to take or choices to make that will lead us back to Heaven, as C. S. Lewis and countless others believe today. Behari, on the other hand gives us a potent and compelling example of what is at stake in our modern world today as far as opening up to or producing soul or inwardness, thereby overcoming solidity. I am far from suggesting that literal traumas are the way to go for us today if we want to rise up to the new level of the consciousness-world constitution, which may be called the soul's interiority *as* interiority, i.e., no longer reflected in nature or substantial forms. Rather, Behari's experience, his gift to us, born out of sustained and horrible suffering, is a record that we can "unpack" to more fully reveal what exactly is at stake for us today, living as we do in our modern world of solid things, in the task of rising up to the level of the next transformation in the evolution of consciousness (perception of the inwardness of what appears to be utter and impenetrable solidity).

The hardness and impenetrability of Behari's experience, with no possibility of escape became for him a true symbol which may be usefully compared with C. S. Lewis (and a host of other authors) who write intelligently and imaginatively about the possible, but as yet not personally experienced, symbolic nature of solidity. For Behari, the rock did open up, it did reveal its interiority. He did experience the inwardness of solidity. Similarly for Merlin, nature inwardized and the background soul reality emerged. But the contrast between the two experiences could not be greater. For Merlin it is a gradual, gentle transition. Natural things: birds, voices, coldness, crevices, isolation, the wind, all gently open to their inwardness, and Merlin simply waits long enough to slide into it. Nature's interiority, at that level of consciousness-world constitution, is still available to the senses, still a given! Nature was, as we would say today, having departed that reality forever, imaginal. For Merlin it is simply "world"!

In contrast, Behari had to experience "no exit", the utter inescapability of his unrelenting situation. Interiority was then produced by the Mind as it inwardized the act of escaping (escaping escape). The new dimension or reality then broke through and Behari could enter it, i.e. his mind could rise up to this new level of reality that was self-produced. Apparently he could then produce it at will by repeating lines of poetry by Leonard Cohen (*The Sisters of Mercy*). Meanwhile, his body continued to be beaten and tortured, as before. It is, unlike Merlin's experience, a condition of extreme contradiction that is a requisite for a fresh perception of the inwardness of solidity today.

On the basis of this description of Behari's account, it appears we must amend and refine our understanding of what outer, material "thing" became, for Behari, a symbol. It is clear that at the "time of Merlin" (i.e., at the level of the consciousness-world constitution pictured in Tolstoy's novel), natural things could relatively easily gain the status of a symbol, as I mentioned above. But is this so with Behari's (or our) experience of the modern world? This is where things get complicated. For Behari, the things themselves (hands, fists, belts, screaming) remained as they in fact are today, secure in their solidity, as Behari knows only too well. He found his way to inwardness (soul) only as an island or perhaps asylum within the larger context of a world of terrorism, religious fanaticism, ideologies, and "steel-and-glass architecture, asphalt streets, airplanes and spacecraft, electronics, computer tomography, shopping malls, etc". [72] Our perceptions/sensations have undergone countless stages of mediations (reflections) over the centuries and into our modern world:

We cannot undo the fact that ours are eyes that have looked through telescopes and microscopes and into television tubes and have been to museums and seen thousands of posters, art reproductions . . . ; ears that have listened to motors, to the rumble of cannons . . . digitalized music. We cannot undo the fact that we know about sound and light waves. I claim that under these conditions the idea of a directly sensible wind [in the way that Merlin, as a picture of the consciousness of our ancient forbears, experiences nature—my insert] *is a cozy idea that misses what is to be seen or felt today, misses* today's *self-display and poetry in the things of nature: the wind, the tree, the bush are rent, scarred, even dead; they are the ghosts of what they once were . . . . Tremendous changes have occurred since the days of mythological man.*

What Giegerich means by natural objects being "the ghosts of what they once were" is that, for us, the "things" have become positive-factual only, or what I have been calling throughout, solid objects in space. They are no longer imaginal, no longer symbolic, or expressive of soul depth (having an aura around them, perceivable by humans in their correlative state of consciousness, as pictured in art etc). We are left to ask where the life of the soul resides today, if not in the things. Nihilism and Existentialism, both gaining ascendancy in the 20th C., proposed that the end of metaphysics is the end of soul, "God is dead"! The appearance of soul, as reflected in substances, had come to an end. Soul apparently has disappeared, but it is a

---

[72]   This quote and the argument that follows are indebted to Wolfgang Giegerich's essays, *The Lesson of the Christmas Tree* and *Effort, Yes Effort!* in (Giegerich W., 2010).

positive-factual error to believe that if the soul has departed the substantial things or natural phenomena, then it no longer *is*.

In order to find the soul in modern life we must "act" in a way that was unheard-of in previous states of consciousness-world constitution. We can no longer simply gaze at the objects and find them "gazing" back at us or speaking to us, granting wisdom, etc. (as we did when nature was alive, with subjectivity). If we gaze at them in that way today then all we see is the positive-factual (soulless) object, that object of the natural sciences. They can no longer be soul phenomena for us, i.e., when gazed at in isolation from the entire world context that we produced and in which the object is embedded in the first place, this including animals, plants, wind and rain—the "ghosts" of our time. Unlike our ancestors, in order to perceive a soul phenomenon, we must become aware of the distinction between the positive-factual object in front of our senses and the medium in which the object arose. For our ancient forbears, the object *was* the medium in which soul reflected itself and thus could become a soul phenomenon. Thus, for example, a singular cleft in a dark hillside could become self-disclosive of "the way down" into Hades. For us, taken in isolation, the same cleft can only be, at most, a geological fault-line, for example, i.e., positive-factual.

With this entire argument kept in mind, we can now return to Behari's account and refine our understanding of the individual experience of overcoming solidity today. I previously said that Behari's breakthrough into the interiority of the soul occurred as an island or, more accurately for him, as an asylum within the larger context of solidity (his beatings etc.) which went on quite untouched by his breakthrough, leaving permanent physical and psychological damage (at least do so in many such cases of trauma). We are now in a position to perceive the entire complex structure of our modern consciousness-world constitution and thus get a fuller, more refined understanding of what overcoming solidity could possibly mean today, for individuals. The positive-factual (solid) nature of the things of the world today is correlative and distinguishable from interiority itself, as interiority. Objects and the soul's inwardness have fallen apart, so that objects, taken in isolation, no longer reflect soul, and yet are still correlative to soul—a contradiction. [73] It seems to be our task to reflect this entire contradiction in our human consciousness, not letting one side fall into the unconscious. Overcoming solidity must mean, then, overcoming (self-transformation of) the entire complex logical contradictory structure that constitutes our world today.

We can say then, that individuals in the unfortunate position of Behari, did not so much overcome solidity as break through into the other side of the contradictory logic of our times. He discovered the soul in its modern psychological status of inwardness itself, but only in the microcosm, as it were. The macrocosm remained, as it does for all us, as solid as ever and he had to return to the macrocosm, as any of us would today. Behari's experience no doubt transformed his life but the entire contradictory soul-world structure today remains as before. His experience, like that of many others today, is a hint of a possible future, as yet not realized in the macrocosm (our shared world, or collective representations).

Other such hints are appearing in a variety of "theatres", among them the arts, literature, and dreams. [74] I had a series of dreams that presented "overcoming solidity" and have dwelled with them for many years, remaining as open as possible to being taught by them. Their phenomenology was quite different from the ordinary dream from which we normally wake up and look back on as over a gulf. None of what happens in the ordinary dream can psychologically reach

---

[73] See footnote sixty-three.
[74] See my book for a fuller discussion: (Woodcock J. C., 2012c).

us anymore and we are left with only memory. These dreams instead emerge in an "in between state" or hypnogogic state and the transition into the dream and back out into waking life is smooth, with full memory and a feeling of continuing resonance with the dream. They are often accompanied by a buzzing sound, like that of bees. In one such dream: [75]

I am lying in bed and I feel familiar deep shudders inside. I decide to go with them, not to wake up and I succeed. I find I can lift off the bed. At first there is a short period of darkness in which I could not see. Then I could see my bed, below. I am up in the corner of the room looking down at the bed. There is a film on my eyes like tears partially cleared but I could see perfectly. I touch the ceiling and find it soft and crumbly as if I could go through it but I decide not to do that out of fear. There is an old light bulb and old decorations on the ceiling. "What are they doing there? That's different from what is normally there." As evidence I decide to unscrew the bulb and bring it down with me to show. I push off the ceiling. There is another period of darkness and I am in bed again.

About ten years passed. During that time I became somewhat familiar with certain symptoms that were indicators of the imminent arrival of another realm of experience, the "in between state". My periodic exposure to these realms had the effect of sharpening the conflict with my daily life, and intensifying my desire for reconciliation. On the next occasion, I again entered the "in between state" awake:

I feel the buzzing, vibrations that seem to signal a shift in reality. Is this the insect storm? I feel fear and let it go. Then I notice my hand is penetrating the bed/earth and scooping through it. Matter has become more fluid as I have experienced before. I push my face through the bed. I can see.

---

[75]   (Woodcock J. C., 2011)

Some effort is needed but the solidity gives way to a more fluid matter. I feel I could, if I dared, go through the wall into my neighbour's apartment. Lack of fear is the key. I feel more ready than ever to do it.

I felt that I had made a smooth waking transition from one kind of reality to another and back again. Ordinary reality and this strange fluid reality were no longer so far apart in experience. Furthermore, I had retained memory of my previous experiences of this more fluid reality. Apparently, I am learning, even though years pass between events.

This was confirmed for me some months later:

I am in bed aware that I am sleeping-yet-awake . . . . Then a kind of magnetic force grips around my ankles, like hands and pulls my feet from below me into the wall so that my feet are suspended in the wall and I am horizontal. If I push and pull, the force would resist like a magnet. I become determined this time to go through the wall and not be held back by fear like the last time. So I push and push until I go through and am on the outside of my apartment, above the ground. I descend slowly to the ground and begin to walk around seeing if it is all the same as in the day time. Yes, but not quite. Then I develop the feeling that I might be making this up, i.e. a doubt and it all became more dreamlike. Simultaneously I am in my bed awake with the memory quite intact.

These dreams had an initiatory effect on me, and indeed, still do. Although they took place in the microcosm, as Behari's did, my perceptions have been broadened and deepened as a result of an ongoing resonance that continues subsequent to the dreams. I am attuned to similar "happenings" occurring to other individuals and, as well, to "developments" in the larger macrocosm. In order to perceive these larger developments, human consciousness must, as I have shown, rise up to the level of the prevailing logic of our consciousness-world constitution today—a world in which the soul has apparently reached consciousness of its own inwardness, along with a correlative external world of solid things, that in themselves no longer carry soul.

With my perceptions thus informed by my own experiences of overcoming solidity, I recently discovered the work of a young artist who also, in her own way, seems to have found her way to the soul's interiority, and found a way to express her discovery in an art form.

Justine Varga did a series of photos of her own studio that was about to be demolished. She said that it became a study of emptiness. She would sit for hours in the empty room seeing nothing, until little by little she would begin to notice things that she did not see before. She tried to render these surprising appearances in her art form: [76]

When I gaze at her photos, I have a strong sense that the space (emptiness) of the room is the focus. The artist seems to be exploring how emptiness, (i.e., the empty space that contains the solid objects of our modern world), at first conceived as nothingness, becomes emptiness now pregnant with meaning, giving birth to appearances or forms (a tiger, a kangaroo, a circle) which she would then render in her art. The forms appear to be emerging from the space, rather than being placed in it. I think what we may have here is a germ of what it looks like to think spatially, i.e., rather than our normal thinking things in inert space. Varga is learning to think spatial thinking: interiority!

Owen Barfield speaks of the evolution of consciousness in terms of the concept of participation. Original participation is

---

[76]   (Varga, 2013)

that form of consciousness-world constitution in which human beings were aware of "an extra-sensory link between the percipient and the collective representations" (their familiar world). [77] They "located" this link "on the other side" behind the phenomena. We may think of Moses and the burning bush in this regards. In no way could Moses regard the numinous light as originating in himself and "lighting" the bush up. Over time, this participation diminished, self-consciousness emerged, and the world suffered an increasing loss of divinity, down to our modern times. Now our modern reality world is as an apparently non-participatory one—our world of solidity. Here, Barfield argues strongly, through vigorous thinking (what he calls beta-thinking), that even today we still participate *our* collective representations, though it certainly appears not to be so. However, we can no longer talk of original participation but of man-centered participation. The origin of the participation lies within us, no longer "on the other side" of the phenomena. For example, the enormous interest in, and study of symbolism (similes, metaphors, symbols) today is one such sign of our participation with the phenomenon, as is the philosophy of phenomenology itself, with its key concept of intentionality. Theories of the imagination, beginning with Coleridge and forward into the tradition of depth psychology, also show a sustained enthusiasm for exploring the way in which we participate the real appearances of the world.

However, this participation is still deeply unconscious. In ordinary life, we simply take it as a matter of fact today that the world of solidity is non-participatory. For example, we take it for granted that the laws of nature run on quite happily without any participation from us. Barfield therefore asks if there are any signs that indicate a movement from unconscious man-centered participation to conscious

---

[77] These quotes and the argument that follows are indebted to Owen Barfield's pioneering work (Barfield O., 1957).

participation, a movement which in effect constitutes overcoming solidity. [78] He points to such signs occurring within Romanticism and in Goethe's scientific work, and as well, the work of Rudolph Steiner. To these examples I want add the work of Gaston Bachelard, particularly his reveries on the elements of fire, water, air and earth. In this book, *Earth and Reveries of Will*, he declares his allegiance to, "the primal and psychologically fundamental character of the creative imagination" which "may precede perception, initiating an adventure in perception". He understands that participation in the phenomenon is only possible through the faculty of imagination, "it is only through the image that the one who imagines and the thing imagined are most closely united". He also agrees with Barfield that this participation is mostly unconscious in us today, when faced with the solid world: [79]

When the real stands before us in all its terrestrial materiality, we are easily persuaded that the reality principle must usurp the unreality principle [the creative imagination—my insert], *forgetting the unconscious impulses, the oneiric forces which flow unceasingly through our conscious life.*

Bachelard notes how, of all the elements, earth (hardness, matter) is the most difficult to apprehend as the creative imagination working "within" the reality of its solidity. For the positivist philosopher and ordinary psychologist, such considerations are out of the question but Bachelard refutes this stance with his understanding of what he calls the "unreality principle," which is "as every bit as powerful, psychologically speaking, as that reality principle" to which we must adapt on a daily basis. This unreality principle, or creative imagination, enjoys an existence of its own, independently of perception. In other words, Bachelard has

---

[78]   Ibid: p. 137 ff.
[79]   (Bachelard, 2002, pp. 2-5)

discovered how solid matter is, along with every other aspect of human existence, an image! But we must be careful here in making the following distinction between literal solid matter and Bachelard's "solid matter". His object of inquiry is the literary earth, not the literal earth. Literary earth images can, as he says, be marked by an explosion of language or imagery, demonstrating the self-referential nature of the creative imagination and its independence from outer literal reality. For example in my own dreams quoted above, there is a clear connection between will and solidity (or resistance), as there was for Behari and in the fairy tales also cited. When my will relaxed in what is known as the hypnogogic state, so too did the hardness of matter (i.e., literary matter, dream stuff) relax and could be penetrated. When Behari's will to escape reached a crescendo against the inexorable resistance (i.e., the psychological resistance in himself—the natural resistance to being beaten to death) that assailed him every day, the Mind involuted, thereby escaping from escape (which can only happen in Mindedness) and inwardness or interiority as such was made, or produced.

Bachelard has given us a formal philosophical account of these fairy tales and individual experiences of overcoming solidity, in terms of the independent existence of imagination. He has shown that solidity may indeed be overcome when we work with what he calls literary images. When we do this in terms of earth or solidity, we find that they become images of resistance with which the will reveals it workings, or aggression is revealed, or terror displayed, or desire to mould, shape the world is released, etc. Literary images are images of earth (in this example) that are already reflected in the mind, taken up as an image in the mind and released (unlike memory) from any reference to the outer world in which solid things remain in their literalness.

We have now, however, reached a status of consciousness that has left the imagination behind and has transcended it altogether. It would not be possible to take up the faculty of imagination itself as an object of inquiry and study unless consciousness was out of it and thus able to reflect on it, as Coleridge, Barfield, Lewis, and Bachelard have done. Another way of saying this is that the soul no longer reflects itself in the things of the world, which, in their very literalness, (by definition having no imagination) are therefore literally solid.

So far, then we have explored what may be called individual efforts in overcoming solidity that characterizes the status of our consciousness-world constitution today. Individuals can experience a spontaneous transcendence from within solidity (Behari); or, as in my case, discover the dialectics of will and matter, or, like Barfield penetrate solidity via the imagination "plus a little bit of will"—what Barfield calls final participation; or, like Lewis and Bachelard, having discovered the objective reality of the creative imagination, choose to play in it, explore its frontiers, enriching our personal psychological lives. At present, all these laudable efforts, as much as they might provide relief from the barren world of hard surfaces that we are faced with on a daily basis, only have relevance for the individual, and maybe for the culture, if that individual chooses to develop some art form or theory that can convey her discoveries to the world, encouraging others to do like-wise. [80]

---

[80] Even though the evolution of consciousness is the cornerstone of Barfield's life-work, he seems to share Lewis' hope for a better future in terms of human beings taking steps to overcome our present status of alienation from nature. For example he suggests a method, based on Goethe's morphological observations of nature, for penetrating to the "inside" of nature, which remains, as Lewis also suggests, as it was before the scientific revolution (Barfield O., 1977, pp. 22-23). Elsewhere, though, he stays faithful to his theory by paying attention to developments in language that seem to suggest a spontaneous movement towards a *return of inwardness* in nature, due, not to human steps taken, but to the evolution of consciousness itself (citation uncertain).

The world remains for all that work, as solid as before. Yet, as I emphasized in the beginning this essay rests entirely on the wisdom-stream that asserts this *a priori*: soul and world are correlative and history is a series of transformations in their dialectical relationship. There *is* an evolution of consciousness (or more accurately, an evolution of the consciousness-world constitution)! Our present consciousness-world constitution is simply the last in a long history of transformations, and so, we may expect, another transformation is underway (or as I said, has already happened at the level of soul) and we are all simply catching up to the "new reality" with our developing philosophies, art forms, individual experiences, and epistemologies in order to make it our truth.

The next question to consider here then is: can we perceive, in the world, beyond this or that individual's accomplishments (or accidents) in overcoming solidity, any movements that demonstrate an objective process of transformation in the present consciousness-world constitution?

THE WORLD'S
SELF-OVERCOMING OF SOLIDITY

To explore this complex question adequately, we must make the distinction between the world in which we live today psychologically and the world in which we live empirically. This distinction did not have to be made in prior stages of the evolution of consciousness, prior to the sharp self-consciousness that we each are today, psychologically. As human animals we share the "in-ness" in life that animals do, i.e., what Jung calls "the universal foundation", or the "great encompassing connection". [81] He goes on to claim that, "From this universal foundation, no human soul is cut off; only the individual consciousness that has lost its connection with the psychic totality . . ." [82] This formulation is very close to Owen Barfield's understanding that we continue to participate the phenomena at all times, while at the same time, our modern self-consciousness is quite cut-off and unconscious of our deeper in-ness in nature. [83]

To get a sense of how this distinction works in our ordinary lives, I want to turn to an art form in which the expression of the distinction between our psychological and empirical lives is the main theme. The movie, *Gerry* (2002), is the story of two young men who travel to the desert for an afternoon of sight-seeing. They quickly get lost and disoriented. The

---

[81] As translated by Wolfgang Giegerich in his unpublished (2013) paper, *Soul and World.*

[82] (Jung, The Collected Works of C. G. Jung, 1970), § 367.

[83] (Barfield O., 1957, p. 35)

movie shows the rapid disintegration of their minds as they are confronted with an alien environment which they try to address, armed only with concepts gained from their familiar technological world: [84]

The simple but penetrating dialogue artistically portrays the enormous gulf between their psychological existence and their present empirical predicament. Prior to the following pivotal scene the dialogue between the boys contains a lot of friendly banter, partly to hide their growing fear. The banter belongs to the world they had been psychologically immersed in prior to their misadventure. It is a world of game shows, video games, and television. Their empirical circumstances only slowly began to penetrate their psychological world and the following scene shows their desperate attempts to address this alien and frightening empirical reality from within their psychological reality (that reality in which we exist as psychological beings).

The dialogue occurs as they are desperate for water and try to work out what to do:

Here, animal tracks. Follow these to water. Animals have to know where the water is. We follow them and they lead us right to the water. Just drink our faces off. Or else they go to the mating grounds y'know . . . and then they mate, and get thirsty and they come back. But I mean . . .

Yeh . . . We don't know how far the water is though and I don't think we should abandon the higher ground idea. Because I think it was good idea and there are rolling hills scattered about and I think if we go on a mountain like Crow's Nest, like that mountain over there . . .

---

[84]   Wikipedia: *http://en.wikipedia.org/wiki/Gerry_(2002_film)*.

Yeh but . . . We know where the water is now. We could just go there and get water and then go on our mountain tops . . . after we get the water . . .

I don't know because what happens if we go to the mating grounds y'know and they see us and get self-conscious and then they don't mate . . .

Then we'll just . . .

And then they won't get thirsty . . .

Then we'll just go there whichever way it is . . . If we go there and it's the mating grounds . . . then . . . we'll just watch them from a brush and they won't know we're there and they won't have any body shame and they'll mate and they'll get thirsty and they'll come back this way and then they'll lead us to the water.

A'right.

And so they proceed into their nightmare.

The two young men attempt (and fail) to address their empirical predicament with concepts and images that belonged to their lived world: nature shows, documentaries, cartoons, etc.

We can see the distinction I am making quite clearly in this dialogue. Although the two boys are empirically in the hot desert, as any animal would be, they (and us modern individuals) are psychologically elsewhere. They are no longer embedded in the great encompassing connection, psychologically. They are outside empirical reality, whereas for animals, the desert is not an alien hostile and frightening adversary. It is more like an extension of their bodies as modern slow-motion camera work by naturalists has shown us—the incredible mutuality for example, between predator and prey. The scorpion does not simply lash out and sting blindly. When it catches it prey in its claws, the stinger slowly comes forward and searches for a particular ganglion in its victim and slowly inserts the venom there, in order to paralyze.

Our ancestors, as animals, lived within the great encompassing connection as well and further, as human animals, lived within what can only be called for humans, world! They were embedded in a living cosmos whose subjectivity and consciousness was unquestioned. Reality for them had not broken into empirical and psychological reality. Our desert ancestors' world, too, was friendly and life-affirming, even if one met one's death there through mishap or mistake. But we no longer live in that world. We have emerged from that world in which soul and habitat were as one. We live now psychologically in what can only be called a technological world, as the two characters from *Gerry* demonstrate so crisply!

We continue to be embedded in the natural habitat, just as animals are and just as our forbears were. But we are no longer psychologically objectively embedded there, quite unlike our forbears. Our world is a technological one as Wolfgang Giegerich notes: [85]

The person with the walkman seems to move through the real world: he is sitting in a tram, he does his homework, he is jogging through nature, and yet in actuality he is totally enwrapped in the music coming at a deafening volume from his walkman and, as far as the soul (not the ego) is concerned, shielded from the external world. One must not

---

[85]   (Giegerich W., 2007, p. 266)

be misled by the external impression that the person with a walkman is in the outside world and as ego may be fully aware of it. In truth, i.e. psychologically, he is inside *the hermetically sealed world of sound, swallowed by it . . .*

The complexity of our modern consciousness-world constitution can now be more fully articulated. On the one hand we live subjectively in a world of solidity, and speak of ourselves accordingly as being substantial selves, separate from the world, with human rights, dignity, worth, and we give priority to our personal free will and choice-making. We can also, as we have seen, overcome solidity, as a temporary personal and real experience, from which we must inevitably return to the same positivistic world of solidity. On the other hand, we objectively no longer live in the world that we subjectively feel ourselves to inhabit. We live psychologically and objectively in the same technological world as the characters in *Gerry* explore so vividly. This is a very complex psychological situation that needs careful elucidation in order to fully grasp the sense in which the world has indeed already overcome its own solidity and taken us with it, whether we know or not.

I allude to our modern psychological situation in the quoted epigram at the front of this book, written by Wolfgang Giegerich, concerning the psychology of the cargo cult of Melanesia. He goes on to say this about our own modern cargo cult. [86]

We are blind to buses and butts in the ashtray, blind to the soul in all the things that come off the assembly line, and doubly blind if we believe to be seeing them . . . . [W]e restrict ourselves to that small and relatively unimportant part of its reality, i.e., to that harmless logical status, that it has in

---

[86] (Giegerich W., 2010, p. 70)

common with natural things (its bodily shape and face), as if the plane were perhaps a kind of bird, the parked bus in the sun something like a big shiny boulder, or what have you. We do not see it together with its sphere (the entire technological civilization with its abstractions, mass production, mass transportation, stress . . .).

Ancient Greek consciousness, for example, could still perceive the outer form of the object as expressive of an immaterial reality. The object was still an image, still imaginal. Thus there was a unity between outer form and soul reality in which Man was embedded at the time. However, embeddedness in nature, i.e., the natural soul (the pantheon of the gods), has come to an end, much to our collective distress. For us, soul reality seems to have disappeared, leaving us only with the positive-factual world (solidity) that we yearn so nostalgically to overcome. We believe that our world and existence has become soulless. But as I said earlier, the withdrawal of soul from reflection in the natural things does not mean it has simply disappeared, this conclusion being an error of the positivist stance (something exists only if it is apprehended through the senses).

Giegerich here and elsewhere shows that the soul has not simply disappeared but has now transformed itself to a logical status that is beyond all form. [87] We are still psychologically embedded in nature, but it is no longer natural nature. It is now our entire technological civilization, i.e., its abstractions: (mass production, global economy, money, the internet, mass communications, media, etc.). We are psychologically surrounded by, and exist within, the soul as we always have (Positivism notwithstanding), except that for us, the soul has withdrawn from substantial form altogether; image no longer

---

[87] See in particular: (Giegerich W., 2007).

is innocently transparent to meaning as it once was, as in the Greeks' *aesthesis*.

I was personally initiated into knowledge of this reality of the modern soul and of our modern existence during a prolonged spiritual ordeal that lasted over twenty years. [88] During this time I felt almost torn apart by the disjunction I felt between my personal inner world which was similar in richness and beauty to that of C. S. Lewis and the outer world which seemed so bereft of meaning and beauty. I bathed in my own psyche, loved it, and felt loved in return, even though some spiritual lessons were hard.

I was also given several dream-visions which unsparingly showed me the objective soul movements, i.e., movements of the world's inwardness, according to the evolution of consciousness. I call them dream-visions to capture the quality of objectivity. They were clearly occurring as "within" me and yet I was "within" them. The inner-outer difference that exists for normal dreaming and waking up had been overcome. [89]

The dream-vision (1991) that taught me the psychological status of soul today as being beyond all substantial form begins:

I am working at a thermonuclear facility along with others. It is the central facility of our society. It is regulated and master minded by central computer, much like HAL in "2001", even to the detail of the red eye with which we could communicate. This computer is female. Everybody thought of her as an IT! In contrast I would look into her eye and talk to her, subject

---

[88] I go into detail of this ordeal in my book, *The Imperative*: (Woodcock J. C., 2011).

[89] For a fuller discussion of this type of dream see (Barfield O., 1977, p. 32).

to subject, with love. In other words, the feminine regulating principle which is the glue of society, by relating all parts to one another and to the whole has become an IT!

But my response alone is not enough. Slowly the lack of relatedness begins to drive her mad with grief. At first, this showed with an increasing, dangerous autonomy in the operation of the objects associated with the facility (society) . . . . elevators going sideways, doors opening and shutting autonomously etc. Then people began to harm one another in various ways until the social system became frayed and anarchy increased with civilization and its values losing cohesion and crumbling.

I find myself in a garbage dump, near the central facility. Some abandoned children gave me a gun to kill them. I take it away from them. A vagabond is sitting in an abandoned car, sewing a boot for the coming (nuclear?) winter. He also used to work in the facility, he said. A sick woman careens by. A man tries to take his twin boys up a tower.

Then I am standing at the centre of the facility. It is ground zero. A large cleared area of gray sand and dirt with concentric rings, like a target, radiating from the centre. The ground is slightly raised at the centre, like a discus, sloping away to the edges. I sense that she is going to explode. I am right at the epicentre. She is going to destroy us all and this means herself in an apocalypse of rage, despair, loathing, hate and grief because of our stupidity. I must get away from the epicentre now. I sprint across the field, down the slight incline to the periphery of the field and sprawl prone, with my head facing the centre, just as she explodes.

The wind starts from the centre and blows out (in contrast to the natural phenomenon which sucks up). It begins as a breeze, increasing in strength and intensity until it becomes an unbearable shriek. Lying face down, I am sheltered by the slope as the wind rips over my back. But I mustn't raise my head at all, a few inches of protection and that's it! Then I know the shriek is hers. I see her standing at the centre, and words emerge, speaking themselves through me:

> *the goddess,*
> *flowing*
> *in her agony.*
> *awesome!*

> *incomparable grief and rage*
> *divine suffering*
> *excruciating pain*
> *such terrible agony*
> *beauty, sublime beauty*

> *how is love possible?*
> *yet this is what I feel.*

A bubble of calm forms around me, while the storm of destruction rages on outside. She is with me in a form that I can talk to. The bubble makes our conversation sound like a small echo chamber. She tells me that because I loved her I may have the boy back (Christopher?). I say, "O! Do you want me in exchange?" I feel quite calm and composed about this. She says, "No, no exchange, just a gift". Then the bubble collapses and the wind shrieks again. Gradually it dissipates and as I turn over, feeling its last tendrils whip at my clothes. I find myself tumbling out of this scene into the everyday world of my daily life. I have been returned from a visionary place to my ordinary life. Then I wake up.

An apocalyptic dream indeed, one that shook me to the core! It has stayed with me all these years (2013), continuing to shape my soul and bring me into accord with the objective soul of the world.

The terrible disjunction I felt between the richness of my personal psychic life and the outer world, seemingly so barren of soul was immediately negated by this dream. I "saw" that the world does have its own interiority and that there is an objective transformation at work. The "goddess of the world" is now the interiority of our entire technological civilization. The apocalypse shows the uroboric nature of soul phenomena: in destroying the things in their substantiality, she is destroying the substantiality of her own nature, i.e., she destroys herself. This process carries the phenomenology of love born out of rage and despair, a love born in the human heart. We can get a hint of the new logical status of soul as all form is destroyed (i.e., as the soul withdraws from reflecting itself in the things), in the poem. The language of the poem is abstract (abstracted from image), conceptual, in the sense of living logic (logos).

I received further teachings about the new psychological status of the objective soul as a reality beyond image, beyond substantial form, in further dream-visions such as this one: [90]

A man was among us, he looked quite normal, like the actor in "Cocoon", except he was alien. He was friendly, wanted to, needed to live amongst us, and was warmly welcomed. Many therapists were excited and thrilled with the glamour of his gifts, which included space ships that could fly at dizzying speeds. I joined in with this madness for a bit but lost interest and instead grew increasingly alarmed.

---

[90]   To see the whole dream-vision and its placement in my twenty-year-long ordeal see *The Imperative*, (Woodcock J. C., 2011, pp. 14-15).

*I tried to warn others, saying, "What if . . . . What if . . . .
?" I decided to act. I wanted to burn him and raced around
looking for a flame thrower. Instead I kept grabbing fire
extinguishers and sprayed him with those . . . useless! He
tried to stop me and we seemed to realize that there was
nothing personal in this. He wanted simply to live here and
I could sense incredible danger to us. I said, "It's just that
our species can't survive if you stay. We need to survive too!"
Then I went back to my frantic search. He said, responding
to my "What ifs . . . ?", "Do you mean, what if I spit on the
carpet or people?" And he did so, thus at last revealing the
danger. A terrible poison was in his spittle, it dissolved flesh
leaving horrible forms, like a fly dissolves its meal . . .*

The dream-vision goes on to reveal a redemptive process but
here we can see how the cold, alien nature of "technology",
i.e. its thinking, has the effect of dissolving substantial form
altogether. It further shows our human fascination with the
technological things, not seeing the "alien" nature of the soul
today. The conflict between the soul's need to enter existence
(the alien's wanting "to live here") and human terror over
the consequences of losing our definition as individuals
(the alien's dissolving our flesh) expresses the complex and
tortured psychological condition as which we exist today. On
the one hand we hang on to our self-definition as persons,
having dignity and worth, being choice-makers, with free
will to live out of our own values, while simultaneously this
same definition of Man as a person is being swept away by
the accelerating advances of our technological civilization.
Instead, a new definition of Man is being cast within our
world, our new nature—artificial nature! Although this new
definition is still being worked out, we can immediately
see how the empirical individual is being rendered
psychologically obsolete within the vast global movements
taking place within our technological world, the world in

which we are embedded today, psychologically, as *Gerry* so artistically portrays.

It is in this sense that the world has overcome its own solidity and moved on into being abstract thought, so alien to the warmth of human values, taking us with it, whether we want to go or not, as indeed the soul has done in all its self-transformations throughout history. This "abstract thought" is not something we do as humans. It is not a "something" at all. We have to conceive of the soul's psychological status today as sheer movement, the spiritual movement of living thinking (logos)—not the kind of movement that things do through positivistic space. It is the kind of sensually impossible movement that is pictured in myths such as those that show the cosmic order in which everything known is surrounded by a stream or serpent that is ever-flowing, never-ending, having no beginning or end, and as well, could have any beginning and end. Any point in the stream is its beginning and end. It feeds itself and empties itself. The logical form of such myths can help us today to see how soul movement, as such, may be manifesting itself today.

We can turn to the Internet; or the flow of Money (24/7 around the world, having no substantial form); or to the shift away from investment in content to the media itself. For example, it no longer matters what image is used in advertising, the only issue being that it sends the message; knowledge in schools has shifted from substantial content to teaching children how to become familiar with all aspects of technological media (Face book, search engines, communication devices, etc.) Children learn fast. They know that if they want to write an essay, they simply have to do a search and download the material that the teacher requires. Becoming familiar with, let alone mastering, the content of the essay is purely a side issue. I once had a discussion with a high level investment manager who was responsible for evaluating companies on the Stock Market, so that investors could calculate the risks. I asked him how long it takes to make his evaluations that have enormous consequences to companies and investors. He told me he has about thirty seconds to make his decisions, so fast is the "movement" of the internet.

We can see here that overcoming solidity is going on at an accelerating rate but is still in positivistic form. Electrons although going around circuit boards at nearly the speed of light still represent abstract thinking (mathematical thinking) as positivistically conceived. So, we must conclude that although the world in which we are psychologically embedded today is overcoming its own solidity, the process has not yet inwardized, at least in its cultural expression. As I said earlier, the soul seems intent in withdrawing from reflecting itself in any substantial form (even image) on the way to absolute abstraction or interiority itself. This emptying out of form seems to carry a phenomenology of rage and despair, as my dream-vision shows but with the possibility of a new form of love breaking through in the human heart. The dream-vision seems to show that if the cold, alien form of soul today (i.e., living thinking abstracted from image) can enter the human heart; an entirely new form of love can break through into existence. Instead, we foolishly and unconsciously identify with the "alien" nature of the soul's abstract thinking and claim it as our own abstract thinking, this time in the sense of dry categories that effectively remove us from our empirical lives. We lose sight of our empirical natures, that nature we share with the animals and "natural nature", thus becoming cold, calculating, able to see "the whole" or the global situation, and having no interest in the individual or the particulars of empirical life. This is not the soul's intent. As my second dream-vision shows, the soul, in its cold, alien status of living thinking, wants to manifest in existence through the human heart. When this can happen, a totally new form of love can enter existence.

It is an extremely difficult to consider how living thinking, which is indeed the overcoming of solidity, abstracted as it is from any basis in the sense-world, could be a form of love when entering the human heart. But apparently we must so consider it.

Perhaps the myth of Semele and Zeus can help us think this mystery a little further. [91] [92]

In the myth (briefly) Semele is impregnated by Zeus and is then tempted by jealous Hera to ask Zeus to reveal himself in his full splendor (the lightning bolt). He warns her but she insists and so is burned up by the vision. Zeus snatches the heart of Dionysos from the flames and consumes it. Dionysos then emerges from the thigh of Zeus as the "twice-born". [93]

Zeus lives on Mt. Olympus but does manifest through earthly natural phenomena: the lightning bolt, the bull, the eagle, the oak tree, and even mortal guise at times. His essential gift is that of fertility when he does manifest but he is also "above

---

[91] With gratitude to the sensitive, soul-centered reading of the myth by Wolfgang Giegerich. See (Giegerich, Miller, & Mogenson, 2005, p. 29 ff).

[92] The following discussion is not to explore the variations and complexities of the myth. I am not a scholar of myth (or much of anything else for that matter). Rather, as I was writing about the logos of the soul, in its modern status as the inwardness of our entire technological civilization, and its connection with love in the human heart, some essential features of this myth occurred to me, i.e., became a soul phenomenon for me, "wanting" to be included here. I immediately "saw" where the evolution of consciousness is leading, or what is trying to be born through this present process of "overcoming solidity" as has already happened at the level of the objective psyche.

[93] (Kerenyi, 1976)

and beyond" earthly life. Dionysos on the other hand is still Zeus, but remains as a spirit *within* natural life: [94]

[I]n Dionysos we encounter a sublatedness of nature [i.e., he was "twice-born" from the thigh of Zeus an entirely "unnatural" birth—my insert] *that nevertheless stays completely within nature, a strictly natural, physical, material sublatedness* [transcendence] *which comes out very clearly in the symbol of wine. Dionysos is a natural, bodily spirituality, rapture, enthusiasm.*

In the writing of this myth I recall a dream fragment I had many years ago, one that seems to belong to this complex of images and thinking, in which I mix rock and champagne together in a glass and drink it down, suggesting that I must assimilate a union between ordinary concrete life and the highest spiritual value from within that life.

In no way am I suggesting that this ancient myth, which belongs solely to the consciousness-world constitution of the Greeks, is a myth of our times but the psychic fact is that it arose in my imagination as I was thinking about the modern soul's negation of all substantiality, in the form of an apocalypse, towards its self-recognition of its own interiority, along with the incarnation of love in the human heart, and I chose to include it simply as an eye-opener to our situation today.

I want to include one more aspect here, again from Giegerich's work on the subject of the myth of Semele as a soul phenomenon. He speaks about a human occurrence that can point to the deeper meaning of the myth: [95]

---

[94] (Giegerich, Miller, & Mogenson, 2005, p. 32)
[95] Ibid: p. 33.

In real life we sometimes find that a great artist has a woman who more or less totally dedicates herself to him in order to serve as his muse. The product of this union, too, is an unnatural birth in that the artist as begetter is at once the one who also himself carries the fruit of the womb to term and gives birth to it . . . as . . . his work of art.

In the "time" of the Greeks the consciousness-world constitution was such that the soul reflected itself in the natural things, and Dionysos was the truth of the inwardness of nature in its ebullient affirmation of life, even in death and dismemberment. At the time of my dream-visions, I was seized by an *enthusiasmos*, lasting for many months, resulting in an outpouring of poetic expression and the invention of a unique art form that could "hold" that expression. Here is a passage from my book, *Making of a Man: Initiation through the Mother*, which conveys some of the quality of my experiences at that time: [96]

For weeks I experienced a flooding of my body with a kind of nectar that produced an ecstasy in me. I could smell flowers or sweet fragrance in the air. I felt I had grown a pair of wings, palpably, concretely. The erotic intensity was such that I would lay down for hours as a fount of glorious liquid fire poured into me. Many dreams came, and visions, too many to recount here but the flood swept away everything that I had so far assumed about Life, the human condition and its limitations. I was given experiences of a concrete nature, whose reality could not be questioned at all and yet which could not possibly be reduced or interpreted back into known categories of experience.

---

[96] For a fuller examination of this period of my life see (Woodcock J. C., 2012b) and (Woodcock J. C., 2011).

These experiences thus have to stand on their own—incontrovertible proof of a reality, discrete yet interpenetrating with ordinary reality. At the peak of my ecstasies, I met a being who I called my beloved Star Sister. She came to me while I was fully awake, alone in my bed. I could get out of bed and see quite clearly with my outer vision that I was alone yet I also saw, felt, and touched her there beside me, as real as my knowledge that I was alone. Both realities were interpenetrating each other. It was then that I experienced myself as being loved by another, totally as an object of divine desire. Here I learned that the human body is able to receive an influx of love from the Beyond. It is the organ of the heart that is the door and it is the self-imposed limitations of the ego that close the door. I felt fearful that I could not contain it and was told again and again by my divine lover that I could, that I needed only to open up completely, right to the level of the cells of my body. I discovered that I could do this and in that condition of complete surrender I received the poetry that came to me.

In considering this complex of images that gather around the core idea of the (soul of) the technological world's overcoming its own solidity, we can see that, like *Zeus and Semele*, there is an apocalypse, a violent destructiveness, and a complete annihilation of substantial form and a revelatory illumination all at once, followed by a birth in the human heart that has the qualities of rapture, enthusiasm, passion, outpouring of ecstatic poetic expression or *poesis*, all taking place, not within the natural nature of the Greeks, but within the artificial nature of our modern technological civilization. Here, Wolfgang Giegerich's quote concerning Dionysos and the artist gives us a further clue as to the nature of the new birth. Could it be that, in overcoming solidity, the soul of the world, in attainment of its nature as interiority as such, as the within-ness of the technological world in which we are psychologically embedded, now seeks manifestation of itself as interiority, through the human heart in the form of a new poesis or dithyrambic expression that carries all the phenomenology of Dionysian "madness"—the ecstatic rapture of passionate expression of life, only this time the soul life of our technological civilization, not natural life (*Bios* and *Zoë*)?

This formulation gets close to the thought of Slavoj Žižek who, walking through a city waste-dump invites us to truly come to grips with our current ecological crisis by refraining from thoughts of returning to our natural roots and: [97]

Not *to break out of this technological manipulative world . . . on the contrary to cut off even more our roots in nature. We should become even more artificial. We should develop I think a much more terrifying new abstract materialism . . . and the difficult thing is to find poetry, spirituality in this dimension . . . to recreate, if not beauty, then an aesthetic dimension in a* [reality] *like this—that's the true love of the world . . . Love is not idealization . . . you see perfection in the imperfect and that's how we should learn to love the world.*

Žižek here is asking us to rise up, in our consciousness, to the level at which the soul of the world is "living" today, i.e., as the syntax of our entire technological civilization, having already overcome all substantial form. We can gain an aesthesis of our world, and it can again become love's expression in actuality. Our modern world as artificial nature can become poetic, as the natural world was for the Greeks through the gifts of Dionysos.

---

[97]   (Žižek, 2013)

Elsewhere I write at length about what such a nature as that of our technological civilization would look like: [98] An aesthesis of our modern world as "the perception of the inner image in the phenomenon, i.e., of the thing with its aura, with the entire 'world' (logical sphere) it represents, not of its positive-factual shape" [99], if determined by the "twice-born" god and his "world", would have to be a "perception" of the fully sensual, life-affirming, animal qualities of ecstatic life, (Zoë)—i.e., of the soul life of our abstract materialism, as Žižek puts it.

It appears that the (soul of the) world's self-transformation has led us to a very peculiar consideration concerning what is emerging from the overcoming of solidity:

How is it possible that the (artificial) world in which we are psychologically embedded today have qualities that belonged to the (Dionysian) world of the Greeks, as well as all prior stages of consciousness-world constitution, where Man was still embedded in natural nature?

---

[98]   (Woodcock J. C., 2012a)
[99]   (Giegerich W., 2010, p. 69)

69

RETURN OF THE "TWICE-BORN"

To find out would require, as Žižek challenges us, a poetic approach to our given world, the artificial world that we have produced. Now would be the time to cast an educated eye into the domain where such an approach may be found, in its infancy to be sure, where attempts are being made to gain a modern aesthetic approach to the artificial world—the domain of contemporary art: [100]

In the 1990's, Chen Zhen, a Chinese artist resident in Paris, made a number of works that recycled the wastes of the Western world—its garbage and its instantly redundant information systems. The pulped remains of the "New York Times" and "Le Monde" became preserved ruins. Other installations consisted of ordinary house-hold settings saturated with mud: the implication being that rampant developmentalism in China reduces its past to frozen archaeological sites . . . .

Chen Zheng's articulated in 1998 a ". . . condition open to everybody in the world today . . . a type of 'cultural homelessness', namely you do not belong to anybody, yet you are in possession of everything. This type of experience itself constitutes a world of its own."

Although much contemporary art is an exploration of our world today it does not seem to want to open us to the sensual, embodied, "Dionysian" life of that world as much

---

[100] (Smith, 2011, p. 259)

as it aims to induce a shock or other strong affect in us, the audience. For example, as I indicate in my book, *Manifesting Possible Futures*, the installation artist Mike Parr subjects the audience to horrors such as having his lips sutured shut to protest Australia's treatment of the boat people (illegal immigrants). [101] Another artist seems to want to provoke sheer revulsion in the audience by appearing to eat a cooked human fetus as his "performance art". [102]

Taken together, these examples indicate the entire domain of contemporary art which, when taken as a soul phenomenon, reflects the logic of our technological civilization: sheer difference; loss of cohesion, values, and any central organizing principle; imagination and feeling (heart) substituted by impressions, sensation, affect; novelty .... All these are the attributes of a world undergoing an apocalypse in which substantiality itself is going under and mediality emerges as the focus of concern.

On the other hand, those art forms that possibly express the inwardness of the artificial nature which we inhabit—its sensuality, animal presence, ebullience, enthusiasmos—its *Zoë*, may not yet exist. I find myself even struggling to articulate what we might look for but the form will have to carry those qualities of natural nature as embodied in the figure of the Greek Dionysos but raised (sublated—see Introduction) to a logical level in keeping with *our* earth, our *artificial nature* as Žižek suggests above.

I think we may expect further hints from the same source that all hints of the unknown future originate—the objective psyche, and our dreams.

---

[101] (Woodcock J. C., 2012c)
[102] (Smith, 2011, p. 160)

Over a long time of paying attention his own and others' dreams, Russell Lockhart writes: [103]

I . . . was struck by what seems to be a gathering tide of apocalyptic dreams . . . I have observed the common elements of an extraordinary event in preparation, a sense of imminence, and . . . a simultaneous and increasing appearance of animals, animals coming, animals, watching, animals speaking, animals wanting to lead us, animals undergoing all manner of transformation.

I can confirm this observation in my own experience. [104] Earlier I spoke of entering a psychological "space" (the hypnogogic state) where I could penetrate matter or overcome solidity in actual (dream) experience. This "in between" state of consciousness also initiated me into other unfamiliar and life-changing forms of existence. Over a period of years dream animals approached me and interpenetrated with my dream body. Their intention seemed to be to "occupy" my sensory-nervous system and experience the incarnate condition (i.e., that peculiar embodied world of the hypnogogic state) through me. A dual kind of consciousness happened in which I remained fully awake (again, in the "in between" state) aware of my human-ness while simultaneously being aware of a psychic *other* also conscious and using my sensory-nervous system. I thus came to know the animal sensual state from within it, just as that animal sensual state also came into consciousness through me: [105]

I am in bed aware that I am sleeping, yet awake. I feel something entering that feels dangerous. I feel the presence of an animal merging with me, co-extensive with my human

---

[103] (Lockhart R. A., 1987, p. 84)
[104] For a fuller description of my experiences see (Woodcock J. C., 2011).
[105] Ibid: p. 19.

form. I move into a crouch position on the bed. I feel rippling power arcing through my chest and my mouth elongates and my teeth are sharp and bared. A growl utters easily from my chest. Power and grace in the animal body yet I am still human, too. I am conscious of my human experience while at the same time I have entered an animal consciousness. The power I feel is exhilarating. I have never felt such freedom. It takes over my speech centres and growls a long basso note with consummate ease. In fact he enters my entire body. All my senses are now available to him.

This extraordinary process of the interpenetration between the human and animal images, occurring on the psychic level, is finding expression in modern literature today. [106] A famous example within the tradition of depth psychology is that of C. G. Jung and the *Leontocephalus*, during his years' long ordeal and engagement with psychic figures, as he recorded in *Liber Novus* or *The Red Book*: [107] [108]

. . . I saw the snake approach me . . . the coils reached up to my heart. I realized as I struggled, that I had assumed the attitude of the Crucifixion. In the agony and the struggle, I sweated so profusely that the water flowed down on all sides of me . . . I felt my face had taken on the face of an animal of prey, a lion or a tiger.

The central aspect of this type of psychic experience seems to be its sensual nature. That is what seems to be insisted upon: the tactile, olfactory, visual, auditory, "immediacy" of the reality in which the interpenetration is occurring. For example, in another such experience I had in 1994:

---

[106]   I explore this theme more fully in my book *Manifesting Possible Futures* (Woodcock J. C., 2012c).

[107]   (Jung, 1989, pp. 90-92)

[108]   (Jung, 2009)

I am a lioness being seduced by a lion. Another lion comes on the scene. We chase him away. Then, as the female, I lick and tumble playfully with the lion who is enjoying himself immensely. I can smell his fur, felt his penis inside me, taste his fur on my tongue (i.e. human/feline tongue)? Was there a feeling that I better humour him so he doesn't see me as human?

Now I have become him—lazy and magnificent. Loping along! I see native people with dogs. I feel my/his immense power as claws dig into a tree and I casually leap up into it out of the way. One dog comes after me but slips back. The men come and below they are talking about fear. Well, what is it that scares you? They ask one. The idea is that by confronting me, the hunter discovers the operation of complexes in his actions, which give rise to fear. So I am the means by which men get initiated.

If we accept the last sentence of this dream as "just so", then it appears that in such dreams it is the soul's intention to initiate human beings into the qualities of living nature, raised to the psychological level of our modern existence, as embedded in (the logic of) artificial nature, or our present technological civilization (mediality, inwardness as such).

The dreams themselves are doing the initiating, unlike the situation of our ancestors in which the animal powers would be invoked physically (for example, a young man would go into the wild and deal with real animals for his initiation). This is because our modern existence is at a psychological level of complexity that has left natural nature well behind as I have already discussed at length. So it appears that after all, natural nature, as well as being left behind irrevocably, has also returned as a more complex, "higher" (not in any sense of "superior") level of consciousness. Hegel's word for this dialectical process is *aufheben*, in which a transformation happens and a necessary death ensues, as well as a rebirth in a totally new form and transcendent level of consciousness. [109]

I propose that these dream experiences of human and animal image interpenetrating, while in a "waking state", are a kind of preliminary initiation into the reality of sublated natural nature, a new nature at the level of image, or, better, Mind, thought—that level of consciousness-world constitution that we have reached today, as reflected in the logic of our entire technological civilization, built as it is on complete abstractions.

How could abstract thought qualitatively *be* as an animal, sensual, alive, present, immediate, instinctual, wild?! We normally think of abstract thought as dry, off the earth, in the air, etc. So a necessary distinction needs to be made here between human abstract thought which is thought that abstracts the general from all the particulars and as such has its reference external to itself in the particulars of concrete existence *and* another kind of abstract thinking altogether. This second kind is the logos of the soul, its life, its self-movement, having no reference to anything outside itself.

Throughout these pages I have been referring to the consciousness-world constitution in which we, as conscious beings, are embedded, reflecting itself in our perceived (i.e., actual) world. I have also pointed to the evolution of consciousness as a series of transformations in this constitution, each resulting in a different status of consciousness with its correlative world. [110] I have further discussed signs that

---

[109] See Introduction. *Aufheben* is translated as *sublation* in English but carries a much fuller meaning that what the English word seems to convey (deny, contradict, negate).

[110] Owen Barfield and Wolfgang Giegerich, and I really mean "a different world", not a different (more exact) perception of the same world that has existed for all time, i.e., the solid world of modernity. My whole thesis here

suggest the soul's life (logos) has already undergone another transformation out of the present positivistic one into (the logic of) interiority itself (mediality)—the logic of self-internal *other*, on the way to the soul's self-recognition as spirit. This shift, I have suggested, is reflected in the world, as the soul's movements always have been. [111] The soul's self-abstraction from concrete substantial things (including images or the imagination itself) results in logos with qualities that include "cold", "alien", "beyond"! But logos has not left the earth, for all this "underworld" phenomenology. Logos was once beyond in the sense of beyond time and space as the Old Testament shows us. Now, it seems that, according to the evolution of consciousness, logos withdrew from natural nature, ascended into "heaven" (or "Mind" as the Greeks discovered, descended into Man, and then through Man back into nature except now, sublated nature, i.e., as the logos of artificial nature, and thence to its telos of discovering itself in its essential soul-nature (interiority, inwardness, negative reality), not as before, i.e., "above", but as the within-ness of, the phenomena of the world (phenomena properly understood in today's context). [112] As Giegerich puts it we are forced to think of the soul's status today as being immanently transcendent, or as being a sensibly given non-sensible. [113]

It is in this sense that the soul (consciousness-world constitution) has objectively already self-overcome solidity!

---

is that solidity also is correlative to consciousness: our modern positivistic consciousness!

[111] "The enemy of psyche is never material things or concrete life unless we forget that these, too, are subject to seeing through": (Hillman, 1975, p. 137)

[112] This is quite a mouthful but, by accepting the *a prioris* of this wisdom-stream (see Chapter 1), these are the conclusions! To further explore the arguments for these conclusions see (Barfield O., 1957), (Giegerich W., 2007).

[113] Ibid: p. 190

There seems to be (if I am reading the auguries aright) that a simultaneous soul-movement is now taking place, into which we may gain insight through the eye-opening myth of *Semele and Zeus* (remembering that this myth "leaped" into my mind as I was writing this book), along with certain strange "dream" experiences that I and others are having today. It seems that the cold alien logos of our times (logos abstracted from all concrete things and yet still within the world, as I said) is now also seeking full, sensual, animal, self-expression in *our* "natural" world (i.e., the artificial nature of our technological civilization). It appears that the logos (living thinking) wishes to express itself in its negative reality in material existence. I have turned to our artists to get a sense of how this could be and suggested that art forms that serve the interests of the "twice-born" (the Dionysian frenzy of abstract thought!) may not yet exist.

There are, however signs . . . [114]

One day the contents of my mind moved faster and faster until they ceased being concepts and became percepts. I did not have concepts about the world but perceived it without preconceptions or even intellectual comprehension. It then resembled the world of UBIK. As if all the contents of one's mind, if fused, became suddenly alive, a living entity, which took off within one's head, on its own, saw in its own superior way, without regard to what you ever learned or seen or known. The principle of emergence, as when nonliving matter becomes living. As if information (thought concepts) when pushed to their limit became metamorphosed into something alive.

With these words, science-fiction writer Philip K. Dick (*Blade Runner*, *The Minority Report*) gives us a glimpse

---

[114]   The following quote is from the back cover of (Dick, 2011).

of an eight year-long immersion into the living Mind. In 1974, he had a revelation which ignited a superhuman feat of writing over a long series of nights, running to eight thousand pages, a "sudden, discorporating slippage into vast and total knowledge that he would spend the rest of his life explicating, or *exegeting*". [115] The posthumous publication of some of these texts highlights Dick's long and arduous attempt to understand what exactly was happening to him. But since he was dealing with "living Mind", and not just his own conscious deliberations, we must conclude that the Mind itself also was trying to understand its own nature in a speculative manner, i.e., mirroring itself endlessly: [116]

I was so clear in my mind as to the exact point in the drama at which we stood: (1) the savior had died, but (2) we had passed over from grieving at the loss (i.e., looking back) but were looking ahead to his return, and rejoicing already . . . . When I think about it, this mood of eager anticipation and expectation and trembling awe and excitement is exactly what the UFO people feel toward the approaching first overt contact . . . . Am I saying the basis of reality is words (or the word) (v.John 1:1), as in Time out of Joint (e. g., soft drink stand, words = ideas = concepts. Ideas in the mind [of God]). Everything points to time travel. And my reconstruction of the fish sign as Crick and Watson's double helix DNA molecule tells me who in the past these time travellers (undoubtedly from the future) presented themselves as.

I chose these passages by simply opening *Exegesis* at random. I want to convey the "sense" of the thinking that took place in Dick's mind, as recorded here. I am struck by sheer movement taking place, on-rushing fervor, a furor, gathering rapids, as syntax begins to overwhelm semantics in the text.

---

[115] From the Introduction, p. xiv.
[116] Op. Cit.: p. 298

I feel punctuation breaking down, or ceasing really to matter, as an onrushing life begins to prevail. I can only "sense" my way as I go along. It's like navigating a maelstrom at times, with little islands emerging only to be swept away.

There is, as yet, no name for this literary style but it does come very close to the process that Lockhart describes as being necessary for us to be led to "imagination's realm". [117]

. . . if we get into the parenthesis, inside those digression, those interruptions of continuity, something else begins to happen . . . a thought intrudes it-self which should of course be in a parenthesis but I can't do it . . . [instead] forget parenthesis all punctuation in fact as poetry has discovered and let everything have its say everything on an equal footing the silly idea mingling with the most profound I once had a dream that I would have to write a paper on the importance of being silly . . .

Russell Lockhart's book, *Psyche Speaks*, was copy-righted in 1982, the year of Dick's death and culmination of his eight year immersion in the living Mind. Lockhart's is a book of auguries and the publication of Dick's *Exegesis* (2011) demonstrates the oracular nature of Lockhart's claim: [118]

Poetry's language is verbs, vital and vivid verbs forcing involvement, inviting relationship rather than separation, immersion rather than distance . . . one can get to the eros in words, the animal in words by discovering the images hidden beneath the shell of words. When you reach this erotic layer in language you begin to experience the poetry in language, the poetry from which words spring, poesis, a fundamental language where psyche and world are one . . . . That way with

---

[117]   (Lockhart R. A., 1987, p. 106)
[118]   Ibid: p. 86-87

language would help us to connect with "the great animals in the background who seem to regulate the world."

Earlier, I pointed to my book, *Making of a Man: Initiation through the Divine Mother* in which I describe my own immersion in this level of language (poesis) during which the sensual (Dionysian) quality of Mind emerged into actuality. I smelled fragrance and tasted nectar, perception became aesthesis, and it was during this time that animal images appeared, seeking interpenetration with me.

My doctoral dissertation comprised a Creative Synthesis along with a Contextual Essay which linked my work to available scholarly resources. My project was a dithyrambic plunge into the turbulent waters of Mind. I simply let go and was caught in a maelstrom. I wrote furiously for about ten days and it was done—no editing was required. But what, exactly, had I done? I even had doubts about who did the doing. It was quite unlike the contextual essays which took weeks of sober reflection and consideration. I completed my degree in 1999 and it is only now (2013), after having read Philip K. Dick's *Exegesis*, that I can "locate" my own work in a larger context. That context is the soul-world's undergoing its own self-transformation—a transformation that involves overcoming solidity and all separation, with the Mind coming home to itself and discovering its own nature *as* Mind, the Mind of the world, in all its particulars, including its sensual, wild nature!

Here is a passage from my Creative Synthesis, which I wrote as a four movement composition and which can conclude the discussion here: [119]

---

[119] From my Finale. My dissertation is available at my website: *www.lighthousedownunder.com*

WORLDS IN COLLISION

Living in the world of the Cartesian paradigm I know that matter is on the outside and spirit is in the inside and that they have an abyss between them. These realities are axiomatic, testable and absolute.

that is until they break down.
until i break down.
until the world breaks up.
when what is so solid crumbles and dissolves,
when what is so ethereal gains flesh and sinew
solve et coagulation

"Our tragedy today is a general and universal physical fear so long sustained that we are used to it . . . we must forget it forever, leaving no room for anything but the old verities and truths of the heart." [120]

are you afraid of weakening my son?
are you afraid of that sweet fire
from fixity to fluidity you go
let it go! let it go! let it go!
i am dissolving father
i am flowing to the sea
i am mingling with another
as the sand swirls on the clear bottom of a wading pool
cicadas thrumming through the night
edges reaching out across space—touching

---

[120] William Faulkner's Nobel Prize Speech in 1949.

they cannot help vibrating
we cannot help vibrating.
iandyou vibrating
resonating youandi
last drop falling falling falling
gone!

I am sitting at a table. A huge wind begins to buffet me. I start shaking as it gets stronger. I reach out and grab our *mani* stone and begin to chant "Om Mani Padme Hum" as the wind reaches a crescendo. I hear in the background a group of Tibetan monks supporting me, chanting too. My body starts up a vibration and I realize that the wind is going *through* my body. It must be a subtle wind! Startling thought! Or, equally startling, has my body changed to become more transparent to the wind? My experience demands the presence of ambiguity.

Head getting hot when I do too much. My skin breaking out again and, burning, burning from the inside. My god! I look sunburned and my face is peeling like a snake shedding its skin. I haven't been outside for weeks on end. Electricity popping my ears and drying out my nose. I feel like a fuse will blow in my third eye. I can't cool down.

I am being initiated by Native Americans . . . the only white man. A ceremonial sacrifice is taking place in which we are placed on the cross and receive cuts on the face and genital. I am also talking with the ancestors who are asking to be released by me. They are trapped. I gain a flash of insight—they seek release into modern incarnation. This holy scene is taking place in the temple of a local garbage dump, the attending priests are tramps and their holy raiments are ill-fitting rags, the sacred objects of veneration are bottles, cans and a gum wrapper lying on the filthy ground with trash, bits and pieces . . . and now I am taken to the Master:

He is a crippled, blind, black man sitting twisted and warped in an old broken wheelchair. His face is the sweet union of a man and a boy. Now I understand how the Deformed heal through direct experience of the deformity. I ask, seeking an oracle from him, "will I live now, what is my future?"

He is seated and I sit at his feet in the dust and kiss his foot tenderly, even familiarly, as if we know each other. He smiles, in love, a feeling of equals. He shows me an oracle, my astrology chart and the houses I have dealt with in this life and the houses I will deal with in the next.

His message is one of love: "Love has broken through in you! You will be all right!" I feel the love, and I go sit in a cafeteria and weep tears of love spontaneously.

When the master loves you, you must die!

I am in my room and I see a door form on the floor. I press on it with my hands. No longer solid but a spongy matter and as I push through the black depths open up and I am dying. I am terrified to go down and I hear thumping below. I also hear the door open and close as alternately I began to relax and fear sets in. My heart is pounding. I remember the countless times I made a temporary descent until I could see something and then I would pop back up with an idea, an image etc. Now I will just go further down. I choose to descend into the abyss and I will not fight it this time. And as I do so, I become blind:

My head is at an awkward angle on the chair. There is a disturbance outside. A bat has landed on the deck, looking directly in. Some black dogs may be chasing him. I struggle to sit upright but my neck muscles are paralyzed. I can't lift my head.

Dr. Jung, as an old man, is in the other chair. People are coming to visit him, while I am sitting on the floor. I ask him about whether he has thought about the point at which psyche or spirit becomes matter (or words become physiological). As I ask I receive an answer from within me: That is the function of the symbol! Simultaneously, Jung nods, "I have and it just so." I relax. He gets up to receive others and strolls into the backyard as I ponder his teaching: how to see in the dark, through vibrations—images formed from sound rather than images formed by light.

The serpent comes, watching me silently from the floor. I close my eyes and remain still. The cobra flicks his tongue in and out of my mouth. As he does so I feel an indescribable feeling of being loved. Then, he leaves.

I feel the serpent rise up my spine, taking over my body—the cobra! I feel his presence within me and outside of me, his huge hood erect and his head and mine concurrent, his tongue and mine one. Yet I feel separate, a witness in awe yet unafraid. His presence is inexorable, I am his vessel and a willing one. I am the medium through whom he works. He sees through my eyes—implacable irresistible hypnotic fate! Head bends over the woman's foot. Tongue touches her leg and there is a flash of light! Her wound is healed. Withdrawing and I leave once again as ordinary as before.

A huge Grizzly bear embraces me from behind. I feel him so close. Such immense power! I can smell him. I cannot flee. He could crush me. We fall asleep together. I gingerly lift a great paw and slide out. As I leave I realize I have left the bear in the house! I start to doubt my actions. Is my fear at the expense of others' safety? I am so sick of being afraid. I return to him and slide back into his embrace. Now I cannot move without taking Grandfather Bear into account.

Now I meet Black Elk and another man. Black Elk has decided to speak and I am very moved by his eloquence. He uses modern psychological language to my great surprise. He says he is no longer going to hold back.

I am beginning to see things that I have not seen before. It's like I have penetrated a veil and can now see how people are behind ethical codes, surface behaviors etc.—what people actually are doing in their lives compared with what they say they are doing. I have received so much condemnation for my own actions that I have not seen others' shadows. Now I am beginning to and I feel disoriented and unstable. My attention is shifted to the bear and what he wants, that is, my concerns are no longer cantered on my ego. There is a duality in my life now.

To be in the bear's embrace is to be alive to the moment, the twist and sudden turns, little predictability. I need to take account of the animal spirit in my actions from now on.

The lion approaches and I become him and he becomes me. I can taste his/my fur on my tongue. Pungent scent fills nostrils . . . loping along on the Savannah in easy long strides . . . natives, people with dogs are coming . . . casually, no fear, claws dig into bark and muscular thighs push up into the crackling branches of a dry tree . . . dog comes, slips, yelps in fear and pain, and crashes down. The men come. They are talking about the lion, teaching the young ones about fear. Yellow eyes watch unblinking and rough tongue idly licks an immense paw of power.

I am with an old man from India. It is night, in his bed. I feel some quivering in my abdomen. It is the same quiver I feel every day now. It literally shakes my body like a spring, often forcing a shout out! I close my eyes and make a decision to surrender totally to this old man.

As soon as I do, I faintly hear him say, "Yes the chrysalis is cracking". Now, I know I have become a butterfly, totally . . . .

I now become in body, totally, an eagle. I can fly though like the butterfly dream, it feels new and strange. Wings stretching, stroking the air slowly and cautiously . . . gliding . . . .

My descent is initiating me into the mystery of image. "Visual" images i.e. based on the eyes with metaphors of light produce an image as object, disembodied and always *over there*. I see a lion—the Cartesian paradigm—subject and object split. I and the lion, self and other forever apart! And so my capacity to see this way was blinded in my descent where Jung offers a teaching and then the serpent, bear, lion, butterfly, and eagle.

Images based on the other senses: ear, tongue, skin, nose, fingers—sensual images—these images gain body and spirit materializes! And worlds begin to interpenetrate, subject to subject.

I am lying in bed and I feel the familiar deep shudders inside. I decide to go with them, not to wake up, and I succeed. I can lift off the bed. At first there is a short period of darkness in which I could not see. Then I could see the bed, below. I am up in the corner of the room looking down. There is a film on my eyes, like tears partially cleared but I can see perfectly. I touch the ceiling and find it soft and crumbly as if I could go through it but I decide not to do that out of fear. There is an old light bulb and old decorations on the ceiling. "What are they doing there? That's different from what is normally there!" But as evidence, I decided to unscrew the bulb and bring it down with me. I push off the ceiling and again there is a period of darkness and I am in bed again. I try to talk but I am curiously paralyzed. With an effort of will, I jerk awake.

I feel the buzzing vibrations that seem to signal a shift in reality. Is this the insect storm? I feel fear and then let it go. I notice my hand is penetrating the bed/earth and scooping through it. Matter has become more fluid as I have experienced before. I push my face through the bed. I can see. Some effort is needed but the solidity gives way to a more fluid matter. I feel I can, if I dare, go through the wall into my neighbour's apartment. Lack of fear is the key. I felt more ready than ever to do it. But not yet! What if I get stuck? Ahh! Fear prevents the interpenetration and keeps the *other* out!

Then I am in bed aware that I am sleeping-yet-awake. I feel something entering that feels dangerous. "Entering" is exactly the right word but "entering where?" is the wrong question. If I say it is entering the room then I am in the Cartesian Paradigm with its certainty of what is inside and what is outside. "Entering me" is more like it as long as I stay ambiguous about the meaning of "me".

The animal enters me and moves into a crouch position on the bed. Rippling power arcing through chest! Mouth elongated with teeth sharp and bared! A low basso growl utters easily, vibrantly deep inside. A crouch that could spring into instantaneous explosive violence! I can feel the full sensual reality of the animal. Then a kind of magnetic field places an iron grip around my ankles, like hands pulling my feet from the crouch position out horizontally behind me so that my feet are suspended in the wall. Mastering a sudden spasm of fear, I experiment. I push and pull, and the force resists like a magnet. I become determined this time to go through the wall and not be held back by fear like the last time. I push and push until I go through and I finally am on the outside of my apartment, above the ground. I descend slowly to the ground and begin to walk around seeing if it was all the same as in the day time. Yes, but not quite. Then I develop the feeling that I might be making this up, i.e., a doubt, and it becomes more dreamlike and simultaneously I return to my body, awake with the memory quite intact.

At last I went through matter. The animal helped me do it—of course! Fear keeps subject and object apart. The animal gave me courage. When my humanness is interpenetrated with the animal, spirit and matter interpenetrate—matter loses its impenetrability and spirit gains body. The wild animal body is the key to the new paradigm!

The image as animal—the key to the new paradigm! What did Jung say? "Why have the animals disappeared from the Christian teaching? When animals are no longer included in the religious symbol or creed, it is the beginning of the dissociation between religion and nature. Then there is no mana in it. As long as the animals are there, there is life in the symbol; otherwise, *the beginning of the end is indicated.*" [121]

In my experiences, image as animal is recovered. I experienced image in full sensual reality. It emerged into ordinary reality through my own senses. I became *other* and *other* entered embodied existence through me—an interpenetration of worlds!

A low basso growl rumbles easily from my lips and I have become a mouthpiece for *other* who enters me in order to become conscious in this world. And so a world is destroyed—a world in which self and other are separated by an abyss—and a new world is becoming through an interpenetration of realities. He comes; he fills my every cell with his presence and he speaks; and thus enters existence,

---

[121] (Jung, 1976)

conscious. I am shaken to the core and when he leaves, my body is a trembling leaf. When he leaves I am returned to my familiar world of duality . . . or am I?

My memory of our encounter is so clear—a full sensual memory! A memory of his smell, the texture of his fur, the easy magnificent power in his body, the memory of his perception of this world. An echo of the image as animal remains with me. A door to his consciousness remains open through this memory. I know I can find my way back there again, with even less fear than before. If called I will answer for I feel a growing obligation in me to do so—Neruda's obligation: [122]

To whoever is not listening to the sea
this Friday morning, to whoever is cooped up
in house or office, factory or woman
or street or mine or dry prison cell,
to him I come, and without speaking or looking
I arrive and open the door of his prison,
and a vibration starts up, vague and insistent,
a long rumble of thunder adds itself
to the weight of the planet and the foam,
the groaning rivers of the ocean rise,
the star vibrates quickly in its corona
and the sea beats, dies, and goes on beating.

Two worlds collide—such generative violence—and there is a becoming. "Life at the core is steel on stone" from which emerges the new form. [123] What we call art is a palpable echo of two galaxies slowly winding through each other over millennia tearing their cells apart with the cosmic force of love yet holding their integrity with spirallic majesty, forever able to carry the memory of that great encounter.

---

[122] *The Poet's Obligation*
[123] (Jung, 1975, p. 119)

John C. Woodcock

My obligation is generated by the pressing down on me of a
    galaxy.
Press down hard on me, break in
that I may know the weight of your hand,
and you, the fullness of my cry. [124]

I am wax upon which the great seal has impressed itself, and thus I am forever changed. The scars I bear in my body are the tattoos prompting memory, entering which I may sing and in so singing a vibration may start up so that you may see a storm on the horizon coming towards you in the heat of a noon-day sun. Your nostrils may flair with a sudden inhalation of dust and the musky sour scent of the power of "cool unlying life" rushing into your blood. [125] With a start you may realize that you do not know if you are afraid or beginning to brim with a strange excitement. Quickening, you do not know whether to run or to hold out your arms in a wild embrace of the *other* who now descends upon you with the passion and ferocity of immediate compelling presence—your own presence—and you will not know whether you are "a bird, a storm or a great song!" [126]

How many flowers fail in wood or perish in the hills without the privilege to know that they are beautiful? [127]

one
i burst forth to greet you, in a paroxysm of joy
yet how often are you gone
i wither and die: where are you?
my sorrow turns to the dank deep earth
i descend slowly
until i meet a surging upwelling of joy

[124]   Rilke: from his *Book of Hours.*
[125]   D. H. Lawrence
[126]   Rilke: from his *Sonnets to Orpheus.*
[127]   Aphorism by Emily Dickinson.

catching me in its wake forcing me
to break forth once more with a silent shout
throwing the doors of my colors wide open
once more to your embrace
two
come, mate with me! make honey!
three
one stray kiss from you thrown carelessly
as you force your way through trees
is enough to gladden me
to ecstasy!
four
why do you rush so, great one?
linger with me. my face will follow yours forever
and when you pass
i will wilt and wither
fade and die
five
what do i want from you?
only this . . .
gaze upon me with all the violence of your desire
until i know who i am in your eyes
six
you are leaving now. yes, i can feel it
you are returning to your restless wanderings
while i remain, my veils in disarray
was it worth it—this all too brief liaison, great god?
i know i touched you
before you withdrew into your silent passage above

AFTERWORD

In my introduction I introduce the word "sublation", drawn from the Hegelian term *aufheben* or *aufgehoben*. In this one word, Hegel successfully conveys the process that I have elucidated here in this book: [128]

> . . . *a sense of a real world out there, subject to Irreversible Time, and thus a sense of irretrievable losses that are at the same time gains; a sense of a possible discrepancy between the logical status our attitude is in* [meaning our private, obsolete beliefs, unresolved positivism, etc.—my insert] *and the status reached by the objective world we produced for ourselves; a sense of many deaths to be died and resurrections to go through* [i.e., as we strive to attain that objective status in our consciousness—my insert] . . .

I suspect that the very structure of my book could be a faint echo of the process of sublation as it worked its way in me. The thinking in the book begins in a formal way within the logic of exteriority in which language refers to a meaning outside itself (philosophical traditions etc.). Then a slow dissolving takes place: memories come, dreams emerge, and associations demand to be included, as if they belonged from the start. The pace of my writing increases and I find myself moving from considered thought to a more, well, I will say it, dithyrambic, self-referential language. I remember quotes from decades ago. I include them without censorship. They always carry a quality of belonging. The thinking takes on a

---

[128]   (Giegerich W., 2010, p. 71)

quality of tumbling, churning vortices, much like rapids in a stream gathering momentum. I simply sit down to write and it tumbles out through my fingers, like right now, a dream presses forth. It is my "Redeemer" dream that I reported above, but as only the first half. It seems that now, the second half wishes to be included. So here it is:

There is a bed of coals, so astoundingly hot that they each glow transparent red. One would simply evaporate on them. In the midst of my passion to stop the alien, a young man, a human, flings himself as a voluntary sacrifice onto the bed of coals. He is the sacrifice who will save us. I am struck with horror and agony, a religious agony that sends me to my knees as I feel his act of sacrifice. O God! O God O God . . . I imagine his flesh blackening and crisping as he rolls on the coals in unspeakable agony. Yet when I actually look, though I am screaming in pain and horror and awe, he is undergoing a different process. He is moving about, but in agony or intentionally? . . . to avoid the heat or to expose himself to it . . . he is not screaming, is he in pain?

He begins to glow red just like the coal itself. He becomes transparently glowing red all over, like a clay vessel does at the highest point that forms the pot. Even more astounding, he is pregnant, almost to full term . . . did he enter the ordeal that way or did the transforming fire engender a new life in him . . . by this time I cannot describe my own feelings at all. It's too much. One cannot name a mystery such as this.

He is our REDEEMER.

FINAL NOTE ON SOLIDITY

The body is solid will. It is frozen will, and we have to thaw it out again. We have to make it our will. And as long as we refuse, or are too weak, to do this for ourselves, physical mortality is called in to help us. Of this we may be sure: if our last death was involuntary, then somehow, somewhere, we shall die again.

Owen Barfield (Death) [129]

---

[129] (Barfield O., 2008)

REFERENCES

Aligheri, D. (1949). *The Divine Comedy: 1 Hell.* (D. L. Sayers, Trans.) London: Penguin Classics.

Bachelard, G. (2002). *Earth and Reveries of Will.* (K. Haltman, Trans.) Dallas: Dallas Institute Publications.

Barfield, O. (1957). *Saving the Appearances: A Study in Idolatry.* London: Faber and Faber.

_____(1963). *Worlds Apart.* Middletown: Wesleyan University Press.

_____(1965). *Unancestral Voice.* Middletown: Wesleyan University Press.

_____(1966). *Romanticism Comes of Age.* San Rafael: The Barfield Press.

_____(1967a). *History in English Words.* Hudson: Lindisfarne Press.

_____(1967b). *Speaker's Meaning.* Rudolph Steiner Press.

_____(1973). *Poetic Diction.* Hanover: Wesleyan Press.

_____(1977). *The Rediscovery of Meaning: and other essays.* San Rafael: The Barfield Press.

_____(1978). *What Coleridge Thought.* Middletown: Wesleyan University Press.

_____(1979). *History, Guilt, and Habit.* Irvington: Columbia University Press.

_____ (1989). *Owen Barfield on C. S. Lewis.* Middletown: Wesleyan University Press.

_____ (2008). Death. *VII*, 45.

Behari, M. (2009, 11 21). *118 Days, 12 Hours, 54 Minutes.* Retrieved from The Daily Beast: http://www.thedailybeast.com/newsweek/2009/11/21/118-days-12-hours-54-minutes.html

Dick, P. K. (2011). *The Exegesis of Philip K. Dick.* (P. L. Jackson, Ed.) New York: Houghton Mifflin Harcourt.

Foldes, K. (2013, 02 03). *Hegel's Deduction of Matter: And the Untenability of the Big-Bang Theory.* Retrieved from Hegel's Science of Philosophy: http://www.gwfhegel.org/Nature/kf.html

Giegerich, W. (2007). *Collected English Papers Volume II: Technology and the Soul.* New Orleans: Spring Journal Books.

_____(2008). *Collected English Papers Volume III: Soul Violence.* New Orleans: Spring Journal Inc.

_____(2010). *The Soul Always Thinks.* New Orleans: Spring.

_____(n.d.). Saban Alternative: An Alternative?

_____(n.d.). Soul and World.

Giegerich, W., Miller, D. L., & Mogenson, G. (2005). *Dialectics and Analytical Psychology: The El Capitan Canyon Seminar.* New Orleans: Spring Journal, Inc.

Graves, R. (1994). *The White Goddess.* New York: Farrar, Strauss and Giroux.

Harris, E. E. (1993). *The Spirit of Hegel.* New Jersey: Humanities Press.

Hegel. (2013, 23 02). *Hegel Glossary.* Retrieved from http://www.london.ac.uk/fileadmin/documents/students/ philosophy/ba_course_materials/ba_19thc_hegel_ glossary_01.pdf

Hillman, J. (1975). *Re-Visioning Psychology.* New York: Harper and Row.

Jung, C. G. (1970). *The Collected Works of C. G. Jung* (2nd ed., Vol. 10). (R. F. Hull, Trans.) Princeton: Princeton University Press.

_____(1975). *C. G. Jung Letters* (Vols. 2 (1951-1960)). (G. a. Adler, Ed., & R. F. Hull, Trans.) London: Routledge and Kegan Paul.

_____(1976). *Visions: Notes on the Seminar Given in 1930-1934.* Zurich: Spring Publications.

_____(1989). *Analytical Psychology: Notes on the Seminar Given in 1925.* (W. McGuire, Ed.) Princeton: Princeton University Press.

_____(2009). *The Red Book.* (S. Shamdasani, Ed., S. Shamdasani, M. Kyburz, & J. Peck, Trans.) New York: W.W. and Norton & Company.

Kerenyi, C. (1976). *Dionysos: Archetypal Image of Indestructible Life.* (R. Manheim, Trans.) Princeton: Princeton University Press.

Lewis, C. S. (2010). *The Great Divorce* (Kindle ed.). Fount, Kindle Edition.

_____(2013, 02 02). *The Abolition of Man.* Retrieved from The Augustine Club: http://www.columbia.edu/cu/augustine/arch/lewis/abolition1.htm#1

Lockhart, R. A. (1987). *Psyche Speaks: A Jungian Approach to Self and World.* Wilmette: Chiron.

_____ (2010). Dreams in the News: Torture, Dreams and Leonard Cohen. *Dream Network, 28*(4), 31-32.

Neihardt, J. G. (2008). *Black Elk Speaks.* Albany: SUNY Press.

Smith, T. (2011). *Contemporary Art: World Currents.* London: Laurence King Publishing.

Solovyov, V. (1985). *The Meaning of Love.* New York: Lindisfarne Press.

Stone, A. (2013, 02 03). *Hegel's Philosophy: Overcoming the Division between Matter and Thought.* Retrieved from Hegel's Science of Philosophy: http://www.gwfhegel.org/Nature/as.html

Tolstoy, N. (1989). *The Coming of the King*. New York: Bantam Books.

Varga, J. (2013, 02 18). *News*. Retrieved from Museum of Contemporay Art: http://www.mca.com.au/news/2012/10/22/focus-primavera-2012-artist-justine-varga/

Woodcock, J. C. (2011). *The Imperative*. Bloomington: iUniverse, Inc.

_____(2012a). *Animal Soul*. Bloomingtom: iUniverse.

_____(2012b). *Making of a Man: Initiation Through the Divine Mother*. Bloomingtom: IUniverse.

_____(2012c). *Manifesting Possible Futures: Towards a New Genre of Literature*. Bloomington: iUniverse.

Žižek, S. (2013, 02 22). *Slavoj Žižek: In The Examined Life*. Retrieved from YouTube: http://www.youtube.com/watch?v=iGCfiv1xtoU

ABOUT THE AUTHOR

John C. Woodcock holds a doctorate in consciousness studies (1999). His thesis articulates the process and outcome of a spiritual ordeal that lasted twenty years. At first it seemed to John that he was undergoing a purely personal psychological crisis but over time, with assistance from his various mentors, he discovered that he was also participating in the historical process of a transformation of the soul as reflected in the enormous changes occurring in our culture, often referred to as apocalyptic. During this difficult period of John's life, he wrote two books: *Living In Uncertainty* and *Making Of A Man*. Both books have been expanded into second editions (2012).

Over time John began to comprehend how empirical or Cartesian reality, seemingly so bereft of soul, is indeed itself a manifestation of soul. Soul and world were found to be a unity of differences. This discovery opened up the possibility of discerning soul movement from within present external reality, comprising hints of the unknown future. John's next three books, *The Coming Guest*, *The Imperative*, and *Hearing Voices*, explore this idea more fully by describing the initiatory process and outcome of a human being's becoming a vehicle for the expression of the unknown future, through the medium of his or her art. John's latest books, *Animal Soul*, and *Manifesting Possible Futures*, establish a firm theoretical ground for the claim that the soul is urging us towards the development of new inner capacities that together he calls the augur-artist mind—the mind that can discern and artistically render hints of possible futures, emerging out of our Present.

John currently lives with his wife Anita in Sydney, where he teaches, writes, and consults with others concerning their soul life. he is also a practicing Jungian therapist.

He may be contacted at *jwoodcock@lighthousedownunder. com.*